INNOCENT CASUALTIES

THE FDA'S WAR
AGAINST HUMANITY

ELAINE FEUER

DORRANCE PUBLISHING CO., INC.
PITTSBURGH, PENNSYLVANIA 15222

The opinions expressed herein are not
necessarily those of the publisher.

ISBN #0-8059-3819-2
Library of Congress Catalog Card Number 96-084493
Printed in the United States of America

Third Printing

For information or to order additional books, please write:
Dorrance Publishing Co., Inc.
643 Smithfield Street
Pittsburgh, Pennsylvania 15222
U.S.A.

or call:
1-800-788-7654

DEDICATION

To the memory of my father, Norman Feuer, who always encouraged me to "take the road less travelled by."

And to my mother, Blanche Feuer, whose love and support has made this book possible.

FDA Updates—1997

JURY ACQUITS PIONEERING CANCER DOCTOR

It's the end of 14 years of war...[and] the beginning of the end of the war on cancer.

Stanislaw Burzynski, M.D., Ph.D.
28 May 1997—Houston, Texas
After his acquittal by a federal jury

For two decades, Dr. Stanislaw Burzynski has had remarkable results treating approximately three thousand patients with his non-toxic cancer therapy—"antineoplastons" (meaning anti-new growth). Despite Dr. Burzynski's unprecedented cure rate, the Food and Drug Administration has spent fourteen years and millions of taxpayers' dollars in its attempt to put Dr. Burzynski behind bars *for life*! The FDA's harassment of Dr. Burzynski is a clear case of the federal government denying Americans access to alternative treatments that work and denying terminally ill patients their constitutional right to freedom of choice in health care.

Stanislaw Burzynski graduated first in his class at the Lublin Medical Academy (Poland) in 1967 and earned his Ph.D in biochemistry the following year. After emigrating to the United States in 1970, Burzynski obtained his medical license to practice in Texas. He worked as a researcher and assistant professor at Baylor College of Medicine until 1977, when he established the Burzynski Research Institute in Houston, Texas.

Dr. Burzynski bases his discovery of antineoplastons—which are short chains of amino acids—on the theory that the body has a biochemical defense system independent of the immune system: "If all of the cancer cells will be reprogrammed and function normally, then, ultimately, we won't have cancer anymore." Since antineoplastons are part of the body's biochemical defense system, they have the ability to inhibit cancer cell growth. This non-toxic treatment has proven to be extremely effective in the following cancers: brain, non-Hodgkin's lymphoma, prostate, stomach, bladder, and kidney. The majority of patients have experienced complete or partial remission or stabilization of their conditions—many tumors disappeared entirely. Moreover, because antineoplaston therapy is usually free of side effects, patients maintain their dignity and quality of life. Not one of Dr. Burzynski's 3,000 patients has filed a complaint against him.

Why, then, has the Food and Drug Administration been at war with Dr. Burzynski since 1983, when it attempted to permanently stop the manufacture and use of antineoplastons?

In March of 1983, the FDA obtained a court order which forbade Dr. Burzynski from shipping antineoplastons across state lines. However, U.S. District Court Judge Gabrielle McDonald ruled that Burzynski could continue to manufacture and treat patients with antineoplastons *in Texas*. This court ruling did not stop the FDA from continuing to harass the Burzynski Research Institute: Agents illegally seized patient medical records and disseminated inaccurate information about Dr. Burzynski and his therapy. When Burzynski applied for an IND (Investigational New Drug) permit to conduct clinical trials using antineoplastons, he was forced to wait six years, until 1989. Most INDs are approved within thirty days. In May of 1997, FDA official Paul Zimmerman admitted in court that the FDA deliberately used "red tape" in its attempt to stop Burzynski from conducting clinical trials.

Was the FDA simply protecting the public from a potentially harmful alternative treatment, as the orthodox medical establishment and most mainstream media would like us to believe? Documented evidence states otherwise: In January of 1988, the FDA confirmed in a letter that it believed antineoplastons demonstrated anti-cancer activity! In 1991, six National Cancer Institute scientists reviewed the records of seven terminal brain cancer patients treated with antineoplastons and concluded that five of the seven had complete disappearance of tumor and two had a partial response. NCI official Michael Friedman, M.D. (who at this writing serves as acting commissioner of the FDA), wrote an internal memo on 31 October 1991, stating that "...Antineoplastons deserve a closer look. It turns out that the agents are well-defined, pure chemical entities...the human brain tumor responses are real."

Although the NCI began conducting Phase II clinical trials using antineoplastons in 1993, the trials were terminated in 1995 after Dr. Burzynski charged that the NCI had violated his protocol. The National Cancer Institute had refused to allow Burzynski to be a co-principal investigator, which would have enabled him to make sure that the tests were conducted appropriately.

Dr. Burzynski's battle with the FDA was just beginning. After *four* grand jury investigations, the FDA obtained a seventy-five count indictment against Burzynski and his clinic in November of 1995: Dr. Burzynski was charged with forty counts of distributing an unapproved drug across state lines, thirty-four counts of mail fraud, and one count of contempt of court for violating Judge McDonald's 1983 court order. If convicted, Dr. Burzynski faced a possible sentence of life in prison.

A mistrial was declared in March of 1997, after the jury deadlocked six-to-six following more than a week of deliberations. Federal District Judge Simeon Lake III dismissed all counts of mail fraud, declaring that the government had not proved its case.

Public pressure was mounting: Dr. Burzynski's patients demonstrated outside courtrooms and lobbied before Congress for legislation that would ensure the right to choose their own treatment. Several of these patients—who had experienced complete or partial remission of their conditions—were interviewed on prime time television. Behind the scenes, FDA lawyers wanted to make a "deal" with Dr. Burzynski: If he paid a fine or at least admitted to criminal wrongdoing, the FDA would rescind all charges. Dr. Burzynski refused.

FDA prosecutors decided to drop all charges except for the contempt count. On 27 May 1997, a jury acquitted Burzynski of the contempt charge since the defense demonstrated that Dr. Burzynski had not shipped antineoplastons to other states.

In March of 1996, President Clinton, Vice President Gore, and former FDA Commissioner Kessler announced at a White House press conference that approval procedures for potential cancer drugs were being expedited. If this were, indeed, the case, why the persecution of Dr. Burzynski? The NCI had verified the safety and efficacy of antineoplastons, approving sixty-eight Phase II clinical trials. With the cancer rate continuing to skyrocket despite President Nixon's declared "war on cancer" in 1971 and more than $29 billion spent on the development of extremely toxic chemotherapy drugs, the failure of conventional therapy was evident and even documented in medical journals such as the *Lancet* and *Scientific American*.

The reality is that the pharmaceutical companies make millions of dollars on chemotherapy drugs, and board members of cancer establishments such as the Memorial Sloan-Kettering Cancer Center (MSKCC) are also board members of the most profitable drug companies: Sloan Kettering's Chairman of the Board of Overseers and Managers, James Robinson III, is also the director of Bristol-Myers Squibb, the world's largest manufacturer of chemotherapy drugs. MSKCC's President and CEO, Paul Marks, M.D., is a director of Pfizer Pharmaceuticals. MSKCC's Vice Chairman, Richard Gelb, is the Bristol-Myers chairman of the board. Another MSKCC board member, Richard Furlaud, used to be president of Bristol-Myers.

Back in 1993, Nicholas Patronas, M.D., chief of neuroradiology of the NCI and leader of the 1991 team that investigated Dr. Burzynski's brain tumor results, stated that he believed Dr. Burzynski's "patients will die" if denied access to his treatment. Patronas was pressured by government officials to withdraw his support of Dr. Burzynski and to cancel the presentation of a paper on antineoplastons, which he was scheduled to present at an international cancer conference in Sweden. However, when ordered to testify at Burzynski's court trial, Patronas admitted, "The basic conclusion was that in these patients the tumors resolved—disappeared. So I think it is impressive and unbelievable."

At present, the Burzynski Research Institute is conducting sixty-eight FDA-approved clinical trials of antineoplastons for various types of cancer, with Dr. Burzynski's patients continuing their treatment as part of the clinical trials. Researchers in Kurume, Japan have independently confirmed some of Burzynski's findings. How many more battles must be fought before Americans have the right to choose their own treatments, before physicians can use safe and effective alternative therapies without the threat of FDA raids and possible imprisonment?

FDA COMMISSIONER RESIGNS

On 25 November 1996, David Kessler announced his resignation as FDA commissioner. During his six-year reign, Kessler refused to acknowledge scientific evidence which supported the use of dietary supplements and alternative therapies for the prevention and treatment of disease. He supported FDA abuse of its law enforcement powers, approving armed raids of medical clinics and health food manufacturers (see Chapter Eight). Since Kessler's departure in March of 1997, Michael Friedman, M.D., has served as acting commissioner.

For the first time in U.S. history, the next FDA commissioner (who is nominated by the president) will have to undergo Senate confirmation hearings. Citizens have the opportunity to lobby congressional representatives and make their preferences known.

LEGISLATIVE ACTIVITIES

The natural products industry and citizen health groups are lobbying key members of Congress in order to protect consumer access to vitamins and herbs and to stop the FDA from its ongoing attempt to regulate dietary supplements as prescription drugs. Although Congress passed the Dietary Supplement Health and Education Act in 1994 (see pages 90-94), the FDA has, once again, threatened to regulate natural foods as "unapproved drugs." According to William Schultz, deputy FDA commissioner for policy, it is the FDA's "tentative judgment" that it cannot adopt CGMP (Current Good Manufacturing Practices) regulations for dietary supplements since "many contain pharmacologically active substances."

There is also an international threat to limit the American public's access to dietary supplements: Codex Alimentarious is a joint United Nations/World Health Organization commission, whose purpose is to create a set of international standards that would "govern" food laws worldwide. An overwhelming number of delegates on the Codex Commission represent international pharmaceutical corporations. As a result, Germany's proposal to create a new Codex standard on vitamins and minerals—which includes controlling the price, dosage, quantity, and combinations of dietary supplements—could be ratified before the end of this century, with vitamins and herbs in therapeutic dosages reclassified as prescription drugs. Under the provisions of NAFTA (North

American Free Trade Agreement) and GATT (General Agreement on Tariffs and Trade), nations which do not follow these standards will face serious international trade sanctions until they make their laws conform to Codex. Worldwide grassroots action is imperative if we are to maintain access to natural products.

The Access to Medical Treatment Act (AMTA), which has been introduced in both the Congress and Senate, would allow licensed health care practitioners and patients to choose alternative therapies not approved by the FDA. If passed, AMTA would educate consumers about the benefits and dangers of medical treatments. Patients who face life-threatening illnesses will have the option to choose alternative therapies when conventional methods fail. Since each state legislates medical practices within its own border, legislation for medical freedom is also necessary at a state level. At present, the following states have medical freedom bills which have been either introduced or passed: New York, Oregon, Oklahoma, Alaska, California, Florida, Indiana, Kentucky, Louisiana, Massachusetts, New Jersey, Ohio, South Carolina, Virginia, Washington, Wisconsin, Nebraska, New Hampshire, Rhode Island, Pennsylvania, Missouri, and Utah.

The U.S. Congress has initiated an investigation into the conduct of the FDA and the Department of Justice. Representative Joe Barton, Chairman of the House Commerce Subcommittee on Oversight and Investigations, has requested all government records on Dr. Burzynski. In addition, members of Congress are expected to vote on FDA Reform Bill (S-830) in 1997, to which Senator Tom Harkin will attempt to attach AMTA (S-578).

REFERENCES

Ackerman, Todd. "Alternative Medicine Gets a Boost." *Houston Chronicle*, 1 June 1997, sec. A, 1, 35.

Blevins, Sue. "Fighting Cancer—and the FDA." *Wall Street Journal*, 2 June 1997, sec. A, 22.

Citizens For Health. *The Natural Activist*, June 1997.

Federal Register. *ANPR re: GMPs* (Advance Notice of Proposed Rule-Making regarding Current Good Manufacturing Practices). 6 February 1997: 5699-5709.

Harris, Suzanne. "Codex Alimentarius: Where it Stands Now? Why it's Important to You!" *Health Freedom News* (May/June 1997): 7.

"Jury in Texas Clears Doctor in Case on Unapproved Drugs." *New York Times*, 28 May 1997, sec. A.

Siegel, Steven. "FDA Set to Jail Pioneering Cancer Doctor." *Health Freedom News* (Nov/Dec 1996): 6-7.

Staff. *The Health Resource, Inc.* Burzynski Research Institute, Inc., 1997.

Tedford, Deborah. "FDA Official: Doctor was Stonewalled." *Houston Chronicle*, 22 May 1997, sec. A, 1.

———. "Jury Acquits Burzynski of Last Remaining Charge." *Houston Chronicle*, 28 May 1997, sec. A, 1, 12.

The Burton Goldberg Group. *Alternative Medicine: The Definitive Guide.* (Puyallup, 1994), 571-574.

Zuniga, Jo Ann. "Jury Picked in New Burzynski Trial." *Houston Chronicle*, 20 May 1997, sec. A, 1, 22.

CONTENTS

Introduction ix
Prologue xiii

PART I
1. True Health 3
2. Evening Primrose Oil —
   "Unfit For Human Consumption" 13
3. True Health's AIDS Test 23
4. The Media —
   An Instrument For Government Propaganda 35
5. Innocent Casualties in a War 41
6. FTC vs. International White Cross 47

Illustrations

PART II
7. The FDA—As Dangerous As the Worst Disease . . . 65
8. An Undercover Dictatorship 81
9. Acquired Immune Deficiency Syndrome 95
10. Political Agendas 107

Epilogue 113
Appendices 121
Notes 147
Glossary 167
Bibliography 169

INTRODUCTION

I became acquainted with Richard Stokley, the president of True Health, Inc., during the summer of 1991, when he was in Los Angeles to discuss True Health's participation in an AIDS documentary. True Health had tested their nutritional supplement in an astonishingly successful 180-day AIDS trial back in 1989. I was researching and developing projects for television, and we met at a production meeting.

Despite the success of True Health's AIDS trial—no other AIDS study involving pharmaceutical or nutritional supplements had produced such positive results—the Food and Drug Administration (FDA) and Federal Trade Commission (FTC) issued a court order to prevent True Health from selling their product as a treatment to AIDS patients. As I drove Richard and his lawyer back to their hotel, Richard related True Health's experience with the federal government. I remember asking, "Are you saying there is an effective nutritional treatment for AIDS and the government is stopping it?" I was appalled.

True Health's AIDS test had been published in the *Journal of Advancement in Medicine*'s Winter 1990 issue. I sent the article to a television reporter, and he forwarded it to the publisher of an AIDS newsletter in Washington. The publisher, who was plugged into the federal government's AIDS network by serving on the board of several AIDS advisory groups, assumed True Health was a scam—he had seen all kinds of fraudulent AIDS treatments and cures. My reporter-friend agreed with the publisher—I was wasting my time with True Health. A vice president at Universal Studios concurred: If the nutritional supplement really worked, it would be easy to get exposure for True Health; all Richard would have to do is latch on to an "AIDS celebrity" like Elizabeth Taylor, or arrange for an interview with "60 Minutes". He could not have been more wrong.

Although the AIDS documentary never materialized, Richard and I kept up a correspondence between Dallas and Los Angeles. *Documented evidence detailing the FDA's and FTC's harassment of True Health convinced me that True Health's story had to be told.*

When I began doing research for this book, I knew as much about nutrition as the average person. I thought that unless you had a specific food allergy, a multi-vitamin and/or three balanced meals a day provided adequate nourishment—I had no idea that vitamins and nutrients could modify or even alleviate chronic illness. In fact, when my aunt, Carol Frank, called to tell me she had relieved a painful arthritic condition through diet alone, I was skeptical. I believed *she* believed she was better, but it was hard for me to fathom that a simple change in diet could cure a chronic disease such as arthritis.

As my knowledge of vitamins increased, so did my knowledge about the FDA's war against nutritional and alternative therapies. The FDA has conducted illegal raids on health food stores, vitamin manufacturers, and alternative health care practitioners: In 1992, FDA agents burst into a doctor's office—guns drawn—to seize Vitamin B! Yet these raids are rarely reported on network news broadcasts or in influential newspapers—the mainstream media is an instrument of the medical establishment.

I learned that bias against alternative therapies goes far deeper than the FDA. The entire orthodox medical establishment—which includes the American Medical Association (AMA), the National Institutes of Health (NIH), the various medical foundations, and the pharmaceutical companies—is threatened by alternative medicine. The conflict between orthodox and alternative medicine has little to do with science and everything to do with economics: If most diseases could be successfully managed with dietary supplements (a projection based on thousands of clinical studies), nutrients would replace the majority of pharmaceutical drugs.

I was given access to True Health files, documents, videotapes, and audiotapes. Pam Chaplin, Lennie Myers, Bill Sanders (pseudonym), Randy Koppang, and Harvey Brennan (pseudonym) were interviewed for the purposes of this book. Statements from Dr. Boyer, Dr. Pyfer, and Dr. Tam—True Health's medical advisors; Dr. Pulse, the physician who conducted True Health's AIDS test; and AIDS test patients were transcribed directly from True Health videotapes.

My appreciation and thanks to Richard, Ann, Mike, and Richard Stokley, Jr. for their generous contributions of time and information. Allan Feuer, James Karnbach, Randy Koppang, and Kirk O'Hara offered their support and encouragement throughout the duration of this project. I would especially like to thank Carol Frank, who drove with me to Texas and never wavered in her enthusiasm and conviction that *Innocent Casualties* would be published.

As long as the federal government continues to support orthodox medicine's monopoly in the field of health, financial and political considerations will prevail over scientific nutritional facts, and medical costs, the manufacturing of hazardous pharmaceutical drugs, and chronic illnesses will continue to escalate.

Freedom *requires* responsibility. Richard Stokley had the courage and determination to stand up to the government, to fight for the health freedoms that are every citizen's constitutional right. Only if more people come forward with the truth will Americans recognize the system for what it is and demand freedom of choice in health care.

June 1995

PROLOGUE

On 14 July 1989 True Health announced the results of their clinical AIDS trial at a press conference held at the Dallas-Fort Worth Medical Center. Although True Health had just reached the mid-point of its 180-day study, the nutritional company decided to go public with its findings since each patient had shown such remarkable improvement in their condition. The implications of the study were too significant to stay silent: By boosting the body's natural immune system with a non-toxic nutritional supplement, AIDS patients could enter into long-term remission.

A few weeks after the press conference, FDA agents Joel Martinez and Ken Davis visited True Health's corporate offices. Despite his previous dealings with the FDA, Stokley assumed the agents had come to congratulate True Health, and that after examining the materials True Health had sent them—a videotape of the press conference and documentation confirming the test results—the FDA would provide federal assistance at this critical juncture.

Yet instead of wanting to expand on valuable research that warranted further investigation, the Food and Drug Administration was prepared to do everything in its power to shut True Health down. The agents presented Stokley with a Notice of Investigation: Martinez, an investigator with the Dallas FDA, led the formal questioning, while Davis, an FDA official with the Texas Department of Health, chimed in on occasion. Robert Williams, Vice President of True Health, was in the room with Stokley during the entire interrogation.

Stokley reminded the agents that True Health had already sent the FDA a videotape and press kit describing the AIDS test. He told them he did not want the FDA as adversaries, that he needed their support in order to make a final determination on the validity of True Health's AIDS test. "Anything you want or need, just ask us and we will provide it for you," Stokley repeated several times during the agents' visit. He explained that although True Health undertook the AIDS study because previous clinical AIDS trials had not involved nutrition, they had not expected a showing of such magnitude.

At first the FDA officials insisted that True Health's nutritional study had been released too soon; they also expressed concern over the amount of money True Health was charging test patients for the product. Stokley told them it was being supplied free of cost, as were the medical tests and Dr. Pulse's services. Whereupon the investigators decided that the nutritional supplement should be classified as a drug since it was a possible "cure" for AIDS. Ken Davis asked Stokley if he wanted to proceed with a drug classification, but Stokley immediately declined. To designate True Health's nutritional product a drug would be as ludicrous as writing a prescription for Vitamin C. Moreover, it takes about twelve years and $231 million to go from the synthesis to the approval of a new drug.[1] *AIDS patients could not wait twelve years for the government to approve a non-toxic nutritional supplement.* Even if Stokley had wanted to have True Health's product classified as a drug, his small company could never have afforded the exorbitant funds.

Stokley presented the agents with True Health's test results and requested, once again, the FDA's assistance so that they could "begin saving lives." Ken Davis replied that whatever worked was fine with him—he didn't care if True Health used peanut hulls in its product.

Davis was determined to talk Stokley into classifying the nutritional supplement as a drug; he even claimed that a couple of items in True Health's supplement could cause the product to be *designated* as a drug. When Stokley continued to resist, Davis retreated to his original contention, that thirty patients were not enough to consider True Health's test a "good study." Exasperated, Stokley explained how the patients'

---

[1] Tufts University reported these findings in 1992. That same year, Congress approved legislation allowing the FDA to charge "user fees" to regulate and review prescription drugs: Fees for new drug applications started at $100,000 in 1992, and will rise to $233,000 by 1997.

overall conditions had improved, and that Dr. Pulse believed ten of the patients would be dead by now if they had not been taking the product.

After scanning a list of all the ingredients in True Health's product, Inspector Davis spotted an unlabeled bottle of aloe vera and said it would have to be embargoed, ostensibly because it wasn't properly licensed by the State of Texas. Stokley offered to set aside the aloe until it was properly labeled, but Davis insisted that the aloe would have to be destroyed. He offered to send Stokley a licensing application for future use. Stokley protested—in his previous experiences with the FDA, it took months to get anything done. The aloe vera was only being used in the test; it was not being sold. He was concerned that the balance of the 180-day test might be interrupted. The FDA officers laughed, saying it wasn't their problem. Seemingly determined to obstruct True Health's AIDS test, the agents detained 283 quart bottles of aloe vera juice for six months until 2 February 1990.

A few days later, Joel Martinez inspected Dr. Pulse's clinic in Grand Prairie, Texas. As he browsed through AIDS test patients' files, he told Dr. Pulse and his assistant, Elizabeth Uhlig: "It is against God's law to save those gays." Martinez later repeated the exact same statement to Stokley. Trying to appeal to an iota of decency that the inspector might have, Stokley asked him about the innocent children and adults who were contracting AIDS through blood transfusions. Our representative from the Food and Drug Administration shrugged: "In a war there are always innocent casualties."

PART I

CHAPTER ONE

TRUE HEALTH

A vast reservoir of health and economical benefits can be made available by research yet to be done on human nutrition.

Benefits From Human Nutrition Research
Department of Agriculture, 1971[2]

The True Health nutritional program evolved as a response to the critical need that exists to improve our level of nutrition. It has been consistently found that patients with serious illnesses have been deficient in certain nutrients, vitamins, minerals, and enzymes; clinical trials and double blind studies document nutritional deficiencies in diseases such as arthritis, cancer, and heart ailments.

The American diet—grocery shelves lined with processed, artificially-flavored, chemically-preserved, pre-packaged food—is notorious for its lack of nutrition. Vegetables are grown in chemical fertilizers and sprayed with pesticides. Fresh foods are exposed to artificial dyes and

---

[2] See Appendix A—"The Benefits of Nutrition"—for detailed information on the Department of Agriculture's study.

chemicals, depleted of most of their nutritional value; exposure to oxygen, heat, light, and water during transportation further erodes nutritional value. When we buy canned vegetables, we are losing more than 50 percent of the Vitamin B_5 and B_6 found in green vegetables, 70 percent of the cobalt from carrots, and 80 percent of the zinc from tomatoes. If the cans are stored for a long time, an additional 25 percent reduction in vitamins occur. And when we buy frozen vegetables, we are losing at least 50 percent of the vitamin content. Depending on the means of preparation, as much as 100 percent of Vitamin C, 60 percent of Vitamin A, and similar amounts in other vitamin categories may be lost in cooking. Eminent nutritionist Dr. George Briggs observed: "The American public is eating a strange diet. We feed our farm animals better, giving them all of the vitamins and minerals we take out of the foods for humans."

Our food decisions are made for us by government and industry: Congress, regulatory agencies, and university researchers are influenced by powerful agriculture and food industry lobbyists. The FDA and AMA have extolled the food production industry on its volume, variety, and value of provisions, to the detriment of the public's health. Modern nutrient deficiencies have coincided with an epidemic of unexplained chronic conditions.

It is thus not surprising that two out of every five Americans are eating a nutritionally substandard diet, eighty million are overweight, and two out of every three have now or will eventually have a chronic medical condition. Unless we buy organic foods or plant our own garden, we must take nutritional supplements to maintain good health.

Richard Stokley has always been aware that nutrition is a problem in today's world. As a boy growing up on a farm in Iowa, he observed that animals put on special diets became stronger and more productive. If improved nutrition was beneficial for animals, it had to be of value to human beings. Stokley studied nutrition at Iowa's Morningside Junior College in the mid-1950s, but it was a traumatic personal experience that determined the prominent role nutrition would eventually have in his life. In 1980, he watched his brother die from bone cancer, just three months after the initial diagnosis:

"I made a decision to try and find a cure for this insidious cancer. Here was a sixty-year-old guy that was in perfect shape, running down the beach with me just a few months before his death. You couldn't tell that there was anything wrong with him. For him to be given this death warrant because of cancer—I made a postulate to try and do something."

And so when a friend of the family told Stokley about True Health's nutritional supplement in 1985, Stokley listened enthusiastically. The True Health product consists of a powdered nutritional supplement (mixed with water) and fatty-acid capsules containing evening primrose oil and fish oil; the key to the True Health program is the internal generation of *prostaglandins*.

Dr. Sune Bergstrom, Dr. Bengt Samuelsson, and Dr. John Vane won the 1982 Nobel Prize in medicine for their discoveries in *controlling* prostaglandins—minute, hormone-like substances. As the basis of an extensive biological system, prostaglandins control all body functions at the cellular level, including: regulating the cardiovascular, reproductive, immune and central nervous systems by controlling the formation of blood clots; influencing the deposition of fat and metabolism; moderating mood changes; shrinking swollen nasal passages; activating the immune system and controlling clotting, inflammation, tumor growth, and allergies.

Essential fatty acids play a vital role in the formation of prostaglandins, as they promote their health and growth. The two main types of essential fatty acids are gamma-linolenic acid (Omega-6) and eicosapentanoic acid (Omega-3). Omega-6 oils come from plant and botanical sources such as evening primrose oil and unrefined vegetable oils, while Omega-3 oils come from fish and marine life. Once fatty acids are depleted, the immune system loses its strength, resulting in disease and chronic illness.

Only in recent years have scientists begun to recognize and understand the importance of essential fatty acids, as the onset of disease is the direct result of a prostaglandin imbalance. *Yet most Americans have never heard of prostaglandins since doctors and nurses are only marginally aware of their significance.*[3]

Stokley first learned about prostaglandins from a videotaped lecture by Dr. David Spears:

"It caught me, this prostaglandin thing. I had not heard of it before, and it was explained to me how prostaglandins work in your body, about the fact that they modulate all the functions in your body. Well, having studied nutrition and having spent a good deal of time in hospitals in the military, it naturally perked me up."

---

[3] See Appendix C for more detailed information on prostaglandins.

What really sold Stokley on *True Health*, what made him decide to investigate the product thoroughly, was the incredible change he witnessed in his mother's health after she started taking the nutritional supplement:

> "My mother was eighty-years-old and suffering from serious rheumatoid arthritis. She was starting to become deformed. When I came across True Health, I took the product to an internist, Dr. Roland White, who, after inspecting it very closely, said it wouldn't hurt her. We put my mother on the product and in two weeks you could see obvious changes. The results were so spectacular it was almost overwhelming. In ninety days she was pain free—the hump in her back disappeared—we couldn't believe it. Here was a woman who really had been unable to walk, and now she was able to do as she pleased.

> "People who knew my mother saw the change in her. She was starting to walk and do things and they'd say 'I want to get some of that stuff!' It really surprised us how much my mother was helped."

Stokley asked his friend, Sterling Miller, to put him in touch with Sterling's uncle, Linus Pauling. Not only did Dr. Pauling validate the information Stokley was learning about prostaglandins, he also introduced him to Dr. David F. Horrobin, one of the pioneers in the prostaglandin-essential fatty acid field.

As founder of the Efamol Research Institute in Nova Scotia, Dr. Horrobin conducts studies and guides nutritional researchers from all over the world. Stokley was invited by Dr. Horrobin to tour Efamol and see for himself the most current work on prostaglandins and essential fatty acids. He was floored by what he saw—time-sequenced photography of the reduction of cancer tumors and alleviation of various disease states through the use of essential fatty acids.

Stokley returned to Dallas with a suitcase full of clinical nutritional studies acquired during his trip to Nova Scotia. His primary goal was to use the research emanating out of Efamol to upgrade True Health's nutritional supplement. By 1986, Stokley owned the majority of shares of True Health, was named chairman of the board, and began running its day-to-day operations.

The first phase of the program, finding people in the medical profession to work with, took several months:

"Let's get the best doctors, do whatever research necessary. Let's not worry about cost. I decided to find the top
people in America to work with, to establish our company
with the medical profession. Through clinical trials and
blood work analysis, we could determine what our bodies
needed.

"I got busy putting True Health together, and had
several doctors—Dr. Smith, Dr. Tam, and Robert Deschner,
Ph.D in chemistry—go to Nova Scotia to meet with Dr.
Horrobin so that we could evolve our product into the best
one possible. Dr. Horrobin very graciously shared with
them all of his knowledge about prostaglandins. The doctors came back realizing we had found something very
viable to human beings. They told me we were on the right
track."

Stokley invited several medical doctors and Ph.Ds to be on True
Health's Board of Directors. John Boyer, M.D., of San Diego, is recognized internationally in medical circles for his work in preventive cardiology and cardiac rehabilitation. From 1970 to 1974, Dr. Boyer was a
member of the President's Council on Physical Fitness and Sports, and
from 1974 to 1976, Chairman of the AMA's Committee of Exercise and
Physical Fitness. Dr. Boyer explains why, for the first time in thirty-five
years of medical practice, he has endorsed a product:

"No other nutritional product that I know of on the
market today provides these essential fatty acids, which are
an important attribute of good nutrition. . . One of the things
I like about this organization, or Howard [Pyfer] and I
wouldn't be associated with it, it's a very ethical, very sin-
cere organization with expert people on its staff."

Howard Pyfer, M.D., a practicing physician for over thirty years,
runs his own clinic, The Wellness Center, in Bellevue, Washington. As
founder in 1968 of one of the nation's first cardiac rehabilitation centers,
CAPRI (Cardiac and Pulmonary Rehabilitation Institute), Dr. Pyfer
observed that good health and increased life expectancy are attainable
through "lifestyle modification—prevention rather than treatment."

Charles Tam, M.D., has specialized in cardiac rehabilitation and prevention of coronary disease for over twenty years. Chief of Cardiology

at St. Helena Hospital in Napa Valley, California from 1973 until 1987, Dr. Tam is at present co-director of the Cardiac Catheterization Laboratory of Lakeside Community Hospital in Lakeport, California. Dr. Tam recalls how he became involved with True Health:

"One of my patients came to me with this product. He said 'Dr. Tam, I know you are nutritionally-oriented. Why don't you take a look at this product and see what you think.' . . . So he brought me some literature. He showed me the product and I looked at it—I studied it—I went to the library—I went back to my biochemistry textbooks. I went to UC San Francisco medical bookstore and bought some more books. I researched some medical journals, read some other people's books and I said, 'Boy, this product has some real merit.' Scientifically, the clinical data is very striking. For instance, I saw papers in which asthma was treated with gamma-linolenic acid very successfully; [as was] premenstrual syndrome, hypertension, high cholesterol, arthritis, multiple sclerosis. And as you look at the data and the basic scientific research, it becomes very impressive."

These were some of the men Stokley would bounce ideas off of, to help him decide in what directions to go with the product. For two years, True Health studied how to blend the various vitamins, minerals, and essential fatty acids for maximum absorption in the human body. If you take essential fatty acids by themselves they are effective, but not nearly as effective as when you combine them with other nutrients.

Stokley:
"We know more about absorption through the human body than anyone else. The British have only studied single substances, but we've studied multiple substances. We've taken all of the nutrients and put them in the proper balance so that all the chemical reactions in your body occur as they're supposed to. For instance, we learned that if you take megadoses of individual vitamins, it can cancel the other vitamins out. We also learned that hard capsules take longer to digest than do vitamins in a liquid form, so we were able to decrease the vitamin dosage in our product."

True Health contains the essential ingredients needed to replenish the body's immune system: a balance of vitamins, minerals, amino acids, enzymes and other key dietary synergizers, in combination with essential fatty acids.

In his patients that take *True Health*, Dr. Tam has noticed a drop in blood pressure and a reduced number of attacks of angina and clotification, and those who have diabetes as well as heart disease have been able to lose weight and lower insulin requirements.

Thirty-year-old Pam Chaplin, who experienced her first multiple sclerosis attack at age sixteen, describes her experience with *True Health*:

"I suffered from very bad attacks each year until I discovered *True Health*. Going up a set of stairs, my legs would give out. At first I didn't think anything of it, but then a couple times my hands would go numb—this happened pretty often. Finally I went to the doctor—a neurologist—who put me in the hospital. He did a spinal test and said I had multiple sclerosis and put me on medication. I was getting really tired and couldn't walk far at all. I could hardly make it across the street. The doctors didn't do anything to help me—they just said it could get worse. I was afraid I would end up in a wheelchair.

"When I get attacks I get paralyzed and put in the hospital, and they pump me with steroids. Sometimes I go numb all over, including my face—it's a nightmare. It's like I'm in another world or something. I don't know what's going on mentally, and once my mind is okay I can't get around physically. It's scary, so scary. The last attack put me in the hospital for twenty-one days and took me six months to recover from. Every time I have another attack it destroys more muscle.

"I was in bad shape—I just felt like lying around—I was about ready to slit my throat. I got off this tranquilizer and was having bad withdrawals, going downhill, when I decided to visit my Mom, who was working in Mexico. I had to be pushed in a wheelchair. The doctor in Mexico said he had treated people with arthritis and AIDS. I was willing to try anything at this point. So he put me on *True Health*, and ever since then it has been unreal. I haven't had an attack since starting on *True Health*. I panic when I get low on *True Health*. Whenever I start to run out of the fatty acids,

I freak out. I've got to get these vitamins, no matter what. I'm scared if I go without them I'll get sick again.

"After I was on *True Health* for a couple of months, I went to my regular doctor and he said, 'Wow, you are sure doing good.' When I told him about *True Health* it didn't even phase him. He refused to believe that the product was responsible for my improved condition. I've been taking *True Health* for five years now, and my health just continues to improve."

Lennie Meyers was forced to undergo a kidney transplant at age thirty-eight, and he started taking *True Health* as a dietary supplement shortly after the operation:

"I take *True Health* for the amino acids it provides. One of the things associated with a kidney transplant is a drug that you have to take, an anti-rejection drug called cyclosporine. It's [cyclosporine] an oil-based medication that has to be taken with a liquid and I choose to use *True Health* as the liquid to take with my anti-rejection drug. So I take *True Health* every day, along with one essential fatty acid capsule.

"I'm probably the only transplant patient in the world who does take it [*True Health*] and I have had success as far as no rejection episodes. I'm extremely fortunate as far as the wellness of my transplant, and my blood chemistry is always exceptionally good. My understanding is that the life expectancy of a kidney transplant is about five years. Since I'm at the five year point, my doctors are watching the function of my kidney. They are trying to determine why it is that some people have rejection and some don't. Now I'm sure that no doctor would say it was because of *True Health*, but there is documentation that *True Health* doesn't affect patients with kidney transplants in a negative way—I'm living proof of that."

About six years ago, when Bill Sanders tested positive for HIV, his doctor recommended that he take *True Health*:

"I started taking *True Health* about six months to a year after I was diagnosed [with HIV]. My doctor introduced me to *True Health*, the fatty acid capsules as well as the drink. I started taking the product twice a day, at that time eight capsules a day, and I've basically stayed pretty much stable for the past six years—no infections, and my blood count has stayed pretty stable. I've suffered no side effects or anything. The only thing that I did gain was weight. I gained about fifteen to twenty pounds the first half year I was on the product, and had to switch over to True Health's *Safe Loss* [nutritional] product, and now I'm still fighting the weight gain. Before I started taking *True Health* I just felt sort of lackluster, with a negative attitude and not a whole lot of extra energy. But the extra protein, minerals, and vitamins in the product really helped, giving me a lot more vibrancy. I started working out again, riding my bike, and so forth."

Because of the encouraging results True Health, Inc. was having—Stokley recalls receiving letters saying, "Thanks so much. If it hadn't been for *True Health* I may not be alive!"—True Health decided to test their product on AIDS patients. But before they could begin their clinical trial, Stokley encountered resistance from the Food and Drug Administration.

CHAPTER TWO

EVENING PRIMROSE OIL—
"UNFIT FOR HUMAN CONSUMPTION"

The Court of Appeals for the Ninth Circuit in the United States has
ruled that, under U.S. law, Efamol's evening primrose oil is an unapproved food additive. This ruling has been made because Efamol's
evening primrose oil contains gamma-linolenic acid, an important
essential nutrient found in substantial amounts in human milk. Efamol
regrets this decision which means that the people of the United States
are to be denied access to this important nutritional substance which is
consumed daily by every breast-fed baby . . . *No country other than the
United States has objected to its sale.*

United Kingdom Press Release—1985

After launching a major marketing plan, including investing in a
video featuring several doctors who had been using the product, Stokley watched as all his efforts started to unravel:

Stokley:
"I was about to make a large sale in California in April of
1988, when agents representing True Health in California
were contacted by a doctor and told to call a certain number
at the FDA to get the low-down on evening primrose oil. A
lady working for the FDA told the agents that evening primrose oil was unfit for human consumption and that it was

banned by the FDA. The agents in California called and told me. I was in shock, so I asked for the number they had called and was given the same story. I lost my agents and any hope of selling the large order we had been working on. Then the FDA, as I have been told, confiscated our supplies (in excess of 100,000 capsules in storage) in the warehouse in Los Angeles, dumping them into trash containers. The warehouse people didn't tell me until a week or so had gone by. I had no idea the FDA was confiscating evening primrose oil."

The FDA had not notified True Health of any pending action prior to the seizure, nor had they presented True Health with a search warrant—the FDA simply seized and destroyed their product. Stokley contacted the FDA branch in Dallas:

"We were more interested in finding out what the problem was and resolving it. I was not looking to be an adversary of the FDA, but I expected them to act in a forthright and honorable fashion. I don't believe they have the right to violate the law. The product they destroyed could have been sent back to the manufacturer and we could have recovered our money."

Agents at the local FDA office told Stokley that evening primrose oil had been on the agency's Import Alert List since June of 1985 because it was designated as an "unsafe food additive." He was astonished. Over 200 worldwide clinical trials had proven its safety and efficacy. American Indians used the evening primrose plant for a variety of ailments, and it was one of the first botanicals exported to Europe (in 1619), where it became known as the "King's cure-all." There is a recorded history of at least 500 years of use.[4]

The evening primrose flower is often referred to as the "wonder plant" because its oil contains gamma-linolenic acid (GLA), an essential fatty acid that is necessary in the formation of prostaglandins. In the

---

[4] See Appendix C for clinical trial data pertaining to evening primrose oil. As a direct result of the Dietary Supplement Health and Education Act of 1994 (see Chapter Eight), the FDA removed evening primrose oil from its Import Alert List on 22 December 1994. [FDA Import Alert #66-04]

standard American diet, the formulation of prostaglandins is blocked by modern food processing (refining, heating, and processing vegetable and seed oils), and by a lack of the necessary vitamins, minerals, and amino acids. Other factors that inhibit prostaglandin formulation are aging, smoking, drinking, taking medication, stress (high blood pressure), and obesity. Essential fatty acids *cannot* be made by the body, and must be obtained from either the foods we eat or from a dietary supplement. *The main sources of GLA are human breast milk and processed oil from the evening primrose flower.*

How could the FDA designate evening primrose oil "unfit for human consumption?" Human mother's milk is the number one source of GLA in the world: It is common knowledge that babies who are breast fed generally have stronger immune systems than those who are not. Japan even adds GLA to their processed milk.

Evening primrose oil capsules are sold over-the-counter in health food shops and drug stores in Canada, most of Western Europe, Australia, and Japan. More than 100 million capsules of Efamol's primrose oil have been sold in Sweden since 1979 and in Canada since 1980. Both countries require governmental registration for certain nutritional products, and consumer complaints made to these governments are passed on to the company. Efamol hasn't received a single complaint concerning the safety of their product in either country. In toxicology tests conducted at an FDA-inspected laboratory (Inveresk Research Institute, Musselburgh, Scotland), high doses of Efamol's primrose oil were found to be nontoxic; two-year carcinogenicity studies were negative as well. Yet the FDA claimed it was unaware of any evidence that established evening primrose oil's safety and effectiveness.

Prior to its removal from the Import Alert List in December 1994, evening primrose oil could legally be sold in the United States as a food or drug only under the following conditions:

1)   if sold as a drug, it was considered a new drug and the responsible person had to submit a <u>New Drug Application</u>;

2)   if sold as a food, it was considered a *food additive*, and a petition had to be submitted to the U.S. Food and Drug Administration.

Although there are many foods commonly consumed that do not have the FDA-specified "Generally Regarded As Safe" (GRAS) status, they are nonetheless safe. However in the case of evening primrose oil, the FDA maintained that its status could only be resolved through a GRAS petition.

Stokley contacted Sherri Clarkson, President of the Efamol Institute, to inquire about Efamol's relationship with the FDA. Efamol Ltd. had already invested $2 million for safety and toxicology studies to meet FDA standards on evening primrose oil. When Efamol tried to defend their position, the FDA refused to look at their extensive clinical trials and literature, nor did the FDA comply with Efamol's legal counsel's suggestion for the FDA to arrange a specific test case.

Clarkson informed Stokley that the FDA had been seizing various quantities of evening primrose oil, black currant oil, borage oil, and fish oil—all essential fatty acid products—from selected U.S. manufacturers. At the same time, these products were still available to the consumer in most health food stores. It seemed impossible, Clarkson told Stokley, to predict what action the FDA would take in the marketplace.

Stokley tried contacting the FDA's Dallas office, and when he could not get a clear answer on evening primrose oil, made numerous calls to federal offices in Washington D.C. After spending several days trying to locate someone there to help him, he finally reached the Speaker of the House, Jim Wright, who called the FDA on True Health's behalf and connected Stokley with FDA Agent John Thomas.

Stokley's June 7th telephone conversation with Thomas was transcribed for True Health records:

Stokley:
"I did not know that evening primrose oil was not on the GRAS list since you could get it in health food stores. I'm getting it from Efamol—I don't want to be caught in the middle of some adversarial goal. Apparently, evening primrose oil was the point of contention. I was trying to find out if there is GLA from another source that wouldn't be hopped on by the FDA—I haven't been able to find out anything."

Thomas:
"That is because such a list does not exist."

Stokley:
"I don't know what to do, and I'm looking to you for advice. I'd like to make an application, but I don't know what all is required. Maybe it costs so much money that it is out of my realm."

Thomas:

"Here's what we've advised others who are interested in this particular substance to do: Either file a food additive petition, or a GRAS affirmation petition—you can submit to us copies of any literature data that would support the safe use of the evening primrose oil or the gamma-linolenic acid as safe for human consumption, in the amounts that you have proposed to use. We will review that data, and either agree with you that the information that you have submitted would support the safe use of this substance at those levels for those purposes, or we will disagree. If we disagree, you still can submit data on a food additive petition, which will include animal feeding studies which will establish that the injection of evening primrose oil and GLA in the amounts that you propose to use would indeed be safe for human consumption. With the successful completion of that kind of petition, we will issue a regulation for human consumption of that particular substance. With that regulation, anyone who wishes to use it will be free to do so; anyone who uses it outside the provisions of the regulation will be in violation of the law."

Stokley:

"If I provide a lot of material with the GRAS application, how much time am I looking at for the review, acceptance and/or rejection?"

Thomas:

"That is indeterminate. We should get back to you within 90 to 180 days."

Stokley:

"I will attempt to do what I have to—the research data that I have has come from various medical schools throughout the world. Would you look at this type of stuff?"

Thomas:

"As long as the information is valid, we're not concerned whether it's foreign."

Stokley:

"It is mind-boggling the work that is being done in this area."

Thomas:
"If the studies support the use of evening primrose oil as a drug, then it might not be valid."

Stokley:
"The studies I have don't indicate it was used as a drug. I have a Ph.D who's helping me. Can he call you?"

Thomas:
"No problem."

Stokley:
"All I want to do is do it right. You have been very helpful. I appreciate it."

Thomas:
"No problem."

Essentially, Thomas was advising Stokley to submit the same information that Efamol—which is world–renowned for its research on evening primrose oil—had attempted to present to the FDA.

Until they could get the evening primrose issue resolved, True Health's proposed clinical trials and marketing program were severely restricted. In the meantime, they had to spend several months trying to comply with all the FDA rules and regulations regarding labeling.

A recently retired FDA agent, Wayne Scrivener, worked with Stokley on True Health labels. Stokley asked two True Health board members, Larry Stowe, who had a degree in biomedical chemistry, and Claude Durham, who had a degree in food chemistry, to explain to Scrivener the importance of GLA in the functioning of prostaglandins. The men also informed Scrivener that linolenic acid, a chemical form of GLA found in soybean oil, borage oil, gooseberries, and evening prim-rose oil, is on the GRAS list. Since linolenic acid had been approved, it only made sense that all forms of GLA should be on the GRAS list. Impressed with what he heard, Scrivener told Stokley that the FDA was out-of-line when it destroyed True Health's essential fatty acid capsules.

Labeling approval had still not been granted when Stokley wrote letters to Jim Wright, to Texas Congressmen Steve Bartlett and Jack Brooks, to Texas senators Lloyd Bentson and Phil Gramm, and to FDA Commissioner Frank Young. In the letters he told of the volumes of evidence which demonstrated that GLA is not only safe, but probably as important as Vitamin C in the daily diet. He even accompanied his let-ters with a current article on GLA, written by a respected medical doctor, James P. Carter, Chief of Nutrition at Tulane University in Louisiana. "What possible reason could the FDA have for calling evening primrose oil unsafe?" Stokley asked the government representatives:

".. . We are an importer and wholesaler of a capsule containing GLA, which is not on the GRAS list. For some strange reason the FDA has seized and destroyed our product and has blocked our importation of this very wonderful product by classifying it as unsafe for human consumption. Our people have met with and proven to the local authorities that this product has been in use for hundreds of years and is completely safe. To require our company to do an FDA-sponsored test to prove the product is safe, or requiring proof that the aloe vera plant is safe, or that sugar cane is safe, to require proof that mother's milk is safe—the product is from a nutritional plant put here by GOD before the FDA was invented."

Although Stokley phoned the FDA office in Washington several times to ask when final approval would be granted, agents refused to take his calls. He asked Jim Wright's office to inquire on True Health's behalf and the FDA insisted that a letter stating the FDA's position on True Health's label had been sent to True Health. True Health never received it. When Wright's office requested a copy of the letter, the FDA faxed one to the Speaker's office; they had still not faxed nor sent the original letter to True Health. An FDA agent told Stokley that he would make sure the letter was faxed to him. It wasn't. True Health only received a copy of the letter via Wright's office.

On 20 October 1988 James Burkel called Stokley with the FDA's decision to detain True Health's operation because GLA was on their label. That same day, Stokley talked to Judy Kraus, who worked in the FDA's Center for Food Safety and Applied Nutrition. She told him True Health had not received the letter the FDA had faxed to Wright's office because it had been lost in the typing pool since September 2nd. Stokley could not believe what he was hearing.

Former FDA agent Scrivener had a suggestion for True Health—simply keep GLA off True Health's label—though he warned Stokley that he would deny telling him this if asked. Scrivener could do something else for Stokley: He could get the nutritional supplement approved by the FDA if True Health paid him $9,000 a month for six months. Stokley, along with two board members who were present in the room—Earl Milton and Larry Stowe—refused to succumb to Scrivener's demands.

The problems continued for True Health, as the FDA detained several thousand dollars worth of capsules in September and November of 1988: "The above-mentioned merchandise is detained by the FDA because it appears to contain an unsafe food additive."

It looked like True Health was going to have to abandon evening primrose oil when the angry shareholders, stockholders, and board of directors elected to fight the government because of the losses the FDA had caused them.

In a letter written on 28 November 1988 to FDA Commissioner Frank Young, Stokley's frustration was evident:

". . . Upon engaging in the business of building nutritional products, one of the first stops made by members of True Health, Inc. was to go to the FDA offices in Dallas to inquire about the proper procedures in complying with FDA regulations. We were never told that we were in any type of violation with the FDA. . . . However, I would like to tell you what we have been facing from the beginning. Your agency violated your own laws by walking into our warehouse in California and ordering our product to be destroyed without proper notification to True Health, Inc. or any officer or member of our organization. We were made aware of this when we called to inquire about delivery and were told the product had been destroyed, and *as yet have not received correspondence from the FDA on this destruction*. . . . True Health, Inc. went to the FDA to visit with Mr. Wayne Scrivener and laid our cards on the table. What are we doing wrong? What can we do to comply? Mr. Scrivener met with Dr. Larry Stowe and Claude Durham to discuss what we need to do to comply. The subject of EPA[5] and GLA was put on the table. The GRAS list was used to point out where we were not out of compliance because of the contents we were using in our product. We made labeling changes and made clear to the FDA that we did not want an adversarial position with them . . . We are again under attack by the FDA—three visits this week from a Mr. Dallas Galbraith of your organization. Mr. Galbraith and his companion came in our place of establishment, searched, *offered no proper papers requesting*

[5] Eicosapentanoic (Omega-3) fatty acids. See Appendix C.

this visit or search, and required several hours of our day. We have had two visits since then and the last visit again took up approximately half a working day. This constant badgering has got to stop . . . If you cannot bring your men into line, I would suggest a congressional hearing to see if we can keep the government out of small business."

The only response to this letter was a telephone call from a Dr. Mason at the FDA, acknowledging that the FDA had received Stokley's letter—there was nothing on paper. In fact, during True Health's entire four-year ordeal with the FDA, none of the congressmen or senators Stokley was in contact with ever replied to him in writing.

It seems that the FDA put evening primrose oil on the Import Alert List precisely because it is a panacea in so many areas of treatment. Efamol's brand of evening primrose oil was available in most health food stores throughout the United States; Stokley had made phone calls confirming this. For some reason, the FDA selected True Health—a company too small to be represented by the special interest groups in Washington—to destroy. What was the FDA afraid of—did True Health's nutritional supplement pose a threat to the orthodox medical establishment?

In order to continue marketing their product, True Health replaced evening primrose oil with linolenic acid on their label. They were now able to focus their energies on a 180-day AIDS test.

CHAPTER THREE

TRUE HEALTH'S AIDS TEST

When lives of people are in the balance, it is totally unethical not to release information immediately.

Dr. Mathilde Krim
Director of American
Foundation of AIDS
Research (AmFAR)

Most of the world first heard of Acquired Immune Deficiency Syndrome (AIDS) during the summer of 1982, when the public was told that Rock Hudson was dying from it. Americans were not aware of AIDS prior to Rock Hudson's last days because the government, medical establishment, and press concealed it. Although the government was privately predicting tens of thousands of deaths, there was no rush to raise money or to mobilize the medical and political establishments. The *New York Times* printed a total of six stories about AIDS in 1981 and 1982. FDA officials doubted that AIDS existed: In December of 1982 they insisted that more proof was necessary before they could enact a new blood policy for the blood banks.

By the time Hudson died on 2 October 1982, 12,000 Americans were dead or dying, and hundreds of thousands were infected with HIV. It was still another three years before the National Institutes of Health, mass media, and community leaders took significant action.

Seemingly uncomfortable with a "homosexual affliction," the Reagan administration ignored mobilization plans from government scientists and allocated little money for AIDS research. The National Institutes of Allergies and Infectious Diseases (NIAID) received $297,000 in AIDS funding in 1982, $63 million in 1986, and $146 million in 1987, compared to almost half a billion dollars in 1990. The President's Commission on AIDS Research sighted a "distinct lack of leadership" from the federal government. In an attempt to educate the nation in public health terms about AIDS, Surgeon General C. Everett Koop released the "Surgeon General's Report on Acquired Immune Deficiency Syndrome" in 1986. President Reagan did not meet with the Surgeon General to discuss the epidemic. By the time Reagan gave his first speech on AIDS in June of 1986, 20,849 Americans had died from AIDS and 36,058 had been diagnosed with AIDS.

In February of 1989, when True Health began their 180-day AIDS Test, AIDS had been researched for about eight years. There was no effective treatment—the disease was just being managed. AIDS kills by attacking the body's immune system, leaving patients vulnerable to opportunistic infections, to viruses that lay dormant until the body is weakened. It is not AIDS that kills people, it is the infections resulting from a suppressed immune system that are fatal. True Health's goal was to improve the quality of life for patients infected with the virus, and to test the *New England Journal of Medicine's* original tenet that AIDS represented little more than malnutrition. Since poor nutrition is one of the risk factors for progressing from HIV seropositive into ARC and then into AIDS, improving the patient's nutrition could possibly delay or put into long-term remission progression of the disease.

The CDC defines AIDS[6] as an infection caused by the human immunodeficiency virus HIV-III. The HIV virus attacks the immune system by invading T4-helper cells, which reduces the body's ability to resist diseases. HIV disease is diagnosed by finding HIV antibodies in the blood serum. Once antibodies have been produced they will remain in the blood—once one tests positive for HIV one will always test positive.

"HIV disease" is progressive, from the initial asymptomatic stage—"HIV-positive," to AIDS-related complex (ARC), and then finally, to AIDS. The average incubation period before symptoms develop is about ten years. ARC is noted for night sweats, weight loss, diarrhea, lymphadenopathy (swelling of lymph nodes), respiratory problems, and abnormal responses of the immune system. The physical manifestations of full-blown AIDS (as defined by the CDC) are opportunistic diseases

---

[6] CDC's definition of AIDS in 1989.

such as pneumocystis carini pneumonia (PCP), Kaposi's sarcoma and diffuse lymphoma (malignancies), AIDS dementia, and "wasting."

In 1989, the primary drug recommended by the CDC for people in various stages of the disease was AZT, as it was claimed it delayed the course of the HIV virus. AZT, a chain terminator of DNA synthesis, was originally developed for cancer chemotherapy to kill actively dividing cells. While the purpose of AZT is to destroy infected T-cells, it kills many healthy cells and is thus very toxic. There are other treatments for the secondary infections that occur as a consequence of HIV disease, but they do not stop the progression of the actual infection.

Stokley recalls his decision to fund True Health's AIDS test:

"Someone said to me: 'If you think your product is so good, why don't you try it on some AIDS patients.' I knew a lot about the wasting syndrome, and I wondered why someone hadn't looked at nutrition.

"So we said 'Let's do it!' Why not try? We had nothing to lose and everything to gain. We felt we had a good chance since most nutritional research is based on single items, while our product encompasses multiple items. It's really quite simple when you look at the chemistry of the body—it has to have an abundance of various nutrients for good health, not just one thing to operate.

"We decided to spend the money, and we found Dr. Terry Pulse, an internationally-acknowledged expert in AIDS treatment research. I showed Dr. Pulse our nutritional research and he became extremely interested."

Dr. Pulse had attended the World Health Organization's (WHO) Global Impact On AIDS Conference in March of 1988 and felt very disillusioned. Nothing was said about nutritional or alternative treatments; it was all politics and money. Three months later, when he presented a paper at the Fourth International Conference on AIDS in Stockholm, he was astounded by the fact that not one of the 9,000 abstracts discussed nutrition. Colleagues attending the conference ridiculed him for experimenting with aloe vera and nutrition in the treatment of AIDS. However, after seeing over one thousand patients stricken with various degrees of the dreaded HIV/AIDS virus, Dr. Pulse was determined to investigate all avenues.

For the clinical trial, True Health supplied their nutritional product and funded the cost of physicians and staff, laboratory expenses, and all of the statistical and computer analyses. The patients were given four times the standard dose of the liquid nutritional supplement and essential fatty acid capsules, along with one hundred percent aloe vera beverage. (The aloe vera did not seem to have a discernible effect, since a second group of patients who were tested without the aloe had test results similar to those ingesting the aloe.)

Dr. Pulse knew that essential fatty acids had been shown to inactivate animal-enveloped viruses. By increasing nutrition while at the same time trying to inactivate the HIV virus, he hypothesized that the immune system might be restored. Thirty-one patients originally signed up for the test, with twenty-nine completing 90 days and twenty-seven completing 180 days. Those who did not complete the test left due to a failure to comply with test guidelines; no one dropped out due to death or deterioration of their immune system.

The test was conducted at the Dallas-Fort Worth Medical Center in Grand Prairie, Texas. Participants underwent a battery of tests that included: in-depth blood screening, complete physical, EKG, CXR, urinalysis, T-Lymphocytes subsets analysis (T-4 helper and T-8 suppressor cells), HIV P-24 core antigen measurement (HIV viral activity level), and a constant comparison of each patient's Walter Reed test scores.

Dr. Pulse:

"I want my research scrutinized but I don't want my patients victimized . . . I came in just as hard-nosed and just as cruel a research scientist as you can possibly put to the task. I had a very strict criteria. I wanted the base line studies on all the patients to include a complete history and physical, a sexual practice questionnaire, and informed consent about what this study would include."

The categories of risk behavior among the patients included homosexuals, bisexuals, IV drug users, heterosexuals, health care workers, and transfusion-acquired. They were encouraged to continue eating their regular diet, along with True Health's nutritional supplement and aloe vera. Since True Health was testing the synergism of nutritional supplementation in addition to what patients were already receiving, participants were allowed to continue taking medications provided by their own physicians. Five of the patients who entered the study were taking AZT. Participants were required to follow safe sex guidelines throughout the study, were tested at 30-day intervals, and could withdraw from the study for any reason at any time.

The Modified Walter Reed Scale, which measures the severity of the disease, is designed to show the progression of AIDS. In theory, Walter Reed scores take in complications and opportunistic diseases, showing the decline of quality of life. The higher the number, the worse the patient. People that test 0 to 1.9 are HIV-seropositive and show antibodies to AIDS but have no signs or symptoms of the disease; those that test 2.0 to 5.9 have ARC and show symptoms of the disease (night sweats, cough, fatigue, diarrhea); and those that test 6.0 to 14.0 have full-blown AIDS.

At the beginning of the test, classifications were made using the Modified Walter Reed Scale: Two patients tested HIV-positive but without symptoms; twelve patients were classified as suffering from ARC; and sixteen patients exhibited advanced symptoms of AIDS. Each patient was also rated at the beginning and end of the test according to the Karnofsky Quality of Life Scale, which is ranked by the patients themselves and is based on their ability to function.

No one could have anticipated the astonishing results at the 90-day mid-point: *All thirty patients who were infected with either HIV or AIDS had shown remarkable reversal and/or remission of their infections; T-4 cell counts doubled and tripled, and many patients were able to function and lead normal lives.*

On the Modified Walter Reed Scale, five patients improved from the AIDS stage to the HIV stage; ten patients improved from the AIDS stage to the ARC stage; ten patients from the ARC stage improved to the HIV stage; and one patient from the HIV stage improved to score zero.

Dr. Pulse was ecstatic:

"As the study started to progress and I started to see Walter-Reeds drop from 12 to 7 to 4.5 to 2.5, and people's function return to where they could get back to work, where their energy came back, where their AZT-induced anemia as side effect disappeared on this only, and not using some of the other drugs that are offered to reverse that—well, I was blown away by the results because they started week to week, month to month, showing such improvement and such remarkable energy levels. But when their T-4s started doubling and tripling, I became astounded. I said, 'What is going on here?' Is it the GLA capsules, is it the nutritional packet supplement, is it the aloe, is it the synergism of all three?"

On a 90-day measurement of P-24 core antigen levels, five patients tested 0, *indicating an absence of HIV viral activity in the body.* On the Karnofsky Quality of Life Scale, eleven patients were rated at the 100 level, indicating normal activity.

The major breakthrough—a strengthening of previously weakened immune systems in all patients and a decrease of HIV viral activity—was mind boggling. No other AIDS study involving either pharmaceutical or nutritional supplements had produced such positive results without any negative side effects. According to Harvard University, only one in five thousand AIDS patients converted from positive HIV activity to negative at the time of True Health's AIDS test.

Stokley arranged for Southern Methodist University to confirm both the Walter Reed statistics and the Karnofsky statistics. Elizabeth Uhlig, RRA, computerized and coded all data, and Phyllis Rueckert, Ph.D., prepared a Statistical Analysis of AIDS Research Data for True Health. Lab tests were performed by Damon Clinical Laboratories in Irving, Texas.

Stokley reacted to the 90-day test results with a mixture of caution and exhilaration:

"We did not have any idea the test would work as well as it did. In thirty days we realized we had stopped the replication of the virus. After sixty days, ninety days—we could not believe the results we were getting. The HIV virus attacks the white blood cells—the key targets are T-4 cells. The T-4 counts had increased—we were affecting the immune system. I called Dr. Boyer and Dr. Pyfer to investigate the study. We were afraid of some kind of fluke, that Pulse didn't know what he was doing."

In order to verify the accuracy of test results and the thoroughness of all procedures, Stokley asked Dr. Boyer and Dr. Pyfer to critically examine all aspects of Dr. Pulse's work. Both doctors confirmed the positive test results.

Dr. Boyer:

"We came to Dallas to look at these records, to meet the physician, and we came with the idea of being critical. And being objective about what we've seen, trying to apply the principles of medical investigation, we have been impressed for a couple of reasons. The first one is that his approach to the patient with well-established AIDS, all of whom have fulfilled certain basic criteria to establish that they have severe AIDS. We have been impressed that his treatment has not been with a drug, that his treatment has not been with some sort of chemotherapy which will damage, destroy and injure tissue, which will make the individual patient feel bad. We have been impressed with the fact that his therapy has been natural, using only nutritional concepts, and we like that because we feel that he is allowing the individual's own body to begin to respond in the right way to the devastating effect of the illness."

Dr. Pyfer:

"I think the big thing that I can see is that the immune system was being jacked up; it was being given the aid that it needed to raise the T-cells back up towards where they were going to be effective, helping to ward off various illnesses. The study also included double-checking on the immune system, to see that the vaccinations would take, to see if the individual could actually build antibodies. So this had a built-in kind of double-checking system. The people not only laboratory-wise got better, but certainly their symptoms diminished and the feeling of well-being began to return. And I saw that all of those [patients] that we evaluated were certainly very pleased with the situation . . . From what I saw and the research we looked at, I didn't see any patient in that group that did not improve substantially, and I think one fellow put it perfectly. He said, 'I now feel that I can wait until a cure comes. Before when I was being treated by the drugs and so on I had no future. But now I can afford to wait because I've got this degree of my health back again.'"

Stokley:

"It looks like we're pretty smart, but we were merely making use of existing knowledge that the medical world bypasses due to their marriage to the drug companies. AIDS patients are lacking nutrients in their bodies.

"People thought our AIDS test was a real long-shot. I was surprised that it was so effective, but since nutrition is the key to the prevention of disease, it makes sense. Some patients were on AZT, but the ones that did the best were not on AZT or any other program. The side effects from our test are weight gain and energy. If I didn't know anything at all, seeing these people before and after tells the story."

Before and after really does tell the story. The experiences of individual patients show that the body's natural immune system may prove to be the most powerful weapon in the war against AIDS.

AIDS TEST PATIENT "E":

"The first symptoms I had when I came in—I was running a fever, I had a lot of nausea, I had numbness in my feet and hands, I had blurred vision, I had rashes, lesions, which—I don't really know what they were, but I was going downhill. Then, I began on this [True Health], and in that first month, the first thirty days, my T-cell count increased sixty points and all my symptoms disappeared. And now, this is my fourth month and I don't have one symptom left, and I'm healthier, I think, than I've ever been.

"I have never felt this good. Even before I had AIDS, I never felt this energetic. And I only need like six or seven hours of sleep a night, and I could never do that before. So I am a real believer that this product is just excellent. It's incredible what the difference has been in my overall health compared to what it was even five years ago, before I even found out about AIDS or knew that I had it.

"I'd like to say that it is very difficult to see my friends that have AIDS that are not doing well, when I am on this product and there is a distinct improvement in my health . . . It is very difficult to be doing this and not have other people have that opportunity to feel better, too. I mean, I know several people that have passed on within the last few months, and it is difficult to see them die when you know that, if they had been taking this product, they probably could have been saved."

AIDS TEST PATIENT "S":

"They determined that I had primary liver lymphoma and at a gathering of the medical clan they said I had no hope. And they put me in the hospital and said I had anywhere from four to twenty-one days to live—they estimated ten days and had me call my family and my attorneys and all that and get everything in order . . . I had seventeen tumors and they offered me chemo . . . I had blown up really big from the chemo and got my weight back down, but my energy level was severely affected. I had to sleep a lot and rest a lot and I had Epstein Barr virus as a side effect. The chemo seemed to exacerbate, I guess, because I would sit down to get dressed and sometimes wake up twenty minutes to four hours later. But after I started this therapy [*True Health*], it just made a huge change in my energy level and my ability to focus my thoughts, because I got lost in a sentence and [now] I feel one thousand percent better. I'm able to do a normal day's work. I'd like to go back to work full-time now. I feel that I can because I'm able to hold my thoughts and produce things and get places, and I've started back to the gym now. They said it would be at least a year after my chemo before I could think about going back to the gym. My T-cells have tripled since I've been on the study . . . I generally feel like ten tons of dynamite now!"

Most of the symptomatic patients reported that within three to five days after starting the nutritional supplement, their energy level improved, fever disappeared, night sweats stopped, cough decreased or stopped altogether, shortness of breath decreased, lymph nodes decreased in size, diarrhea stopped and weakness improved. Many AIDS patients die of starvation because of decreased food intake, malabsorption, or metabolic alterations. During True Health's AIDS test, diarrhea stopped and wasting reversed in all affected patients. There was even, at the end of the study, a 7 percent average weight gain, and patients with anemia induced by AZT all showed marked improvements.

AIDS TEST PATIENT "D" compared his experience with AZT to that of *True Health*:

"I started taking the AZT and started to have some bad reactions to it. I was getting severe—not headaches, but just like a continuous pressure on my brain; I mean, like, as if someone had a vise on it. Plus, I was getting worse as far as upset stomach and all that, and I reached a point after about four days of taking it that one morning I woke up and I had dry heaves. I don't know. I've had medicine before and I felt like this was very toxic."

When a friend referred him to Dr. Pulse, PATIENT "D" jumped at the chance to participate in True Health's AIDS test:

"At the time he [Dr. Pulse] looked at me I was still having—I have hairy leukoplakia on my tongue—and then the experimental program [AIDS test] came into effect two months ago . . . My energy levels are much higher. I feel a lot better. I mean, I don't run into the fatigue that I was running into. I would come home some nights from work just wanting to go to sleep. I mean, I was tired. I just had no energy. But basically overall, I have a lot more energy."

During the 180-day test, the overall quality of life for each patient improved at all stages of the disease. As their immune systems became stronger and more effective, the viral population decreased, enabling them to fight foreign invaders. As Stokley noted, the only side effects were weight gain and increased energy.

One theory for the high success rate of True Health's AIDS test is the possibility that AIDS patients lack essential fatty acids. In the 15 April 1985 issue of the *Canadian Medical Association Journal*, Dr. U.N. Das hypothesized that essential fatty acid deficiency could be one of the predisposing factors for AIDS. Dr. Das speculated that the high incidence of Kaposi's sarcoma, immunodeficiency, and seborrheic dermatitis in AIDS patients were directly caused by an absence of essential fatty acids. Since prostaglandins are critical to the functioning of the immune system, it is plausible that essential fatty acid deficiency could determine one's susceptibility to AIDS. Clinical trials have demonstrated the dramatic effect essential fatty acids have on other immune-deficiency diseases such as multiple sclerosis and rheumatoid arthritis (see Appendix C).

Malnutrition is common in people who are HIV-positive and almost universal in people with AIDS. In the long-term management of the AIDS patient, nutritional supplementation seems to be the most viable and positive course of action to pursue. Dr. Boyer concurs:

"If we don't do something like this, the economic impact at the national level—trying to help over years the progressively debilitated AIDS patient—is going to be staggering. Anything that we can do to help the individual rebuild some of his own protective mechanisms with a non–harmful product like nutrition, like vitamin supplementation, like antioxidants, like essential fatty acids—we have everything to gain by doing this and nothing to lose."

CHAPTER FOUR

THE MEDIA - AN INSTRUMENT FOR GOVERNMENT PROPAGANDA

The word 'free' still existed in Newspeak, but it could only be used in such statements as 'This dog is free from lice' or 'This field is free from weeds'. It could not be used in its old sense of 'politically free' or 'intellectually free' since political and intellectual freedom no longer existed even as concepts, and were therefore of necessity nameless.

George Orwell
1984

Upon the advice of his highly-respected medical advisors, John Boyer and Howard Pyfer, Stokley decided to hold a press conference midway through the 180-day test:

> "We were not going to release this information at the end of ninety days, but the results were so spectacular we thought maybe we had better. After the doctors investigated Pulse's research, which included checking the blood work and interviewing the patients, they were absolutely amazed and said we owed it to the public to go to the press."

Press conference invitations were sent to the following news organizations: ABC, NBC, and CBS affiliates in Dallas; KTVT and KERA in Dallas; the *Dallas Morning News*, the *Dallas Times Herald*, and the *Fort Worth Star Telegram*; Associated Press; TWN Communications, Inc.; *Texas Woman's News*; *Wichita Falls Times Record*; radio stations KRLD and KLIF; and to FDA offices in Maryland and Dallas.

On 14 July 1989, Dr. Pulse announced the test results at the Dallas-Fort Worth Medical Center. Stokley instructed the doctors and AIDS patients to "tell it like it is." True Health invited serious inquiry into their company, its product, and the AIDS study, making available to reporters all of the pertinent files.

Yet to True Health's shock and dismay, not only did the news media refuse to investigate their AIDS study, most of the media didn't even bother to report it. Three weeks after the press conference, there were only two published articles, in the *Dallas Morning News* and in the *Witchita Falls Times Record*. The *Dallas Morning News* article contained mis-statements that were intended to cast aspersions on both the study and True Health.

Sherry Jacobson, the reporter from the *Dallas Morning News*, wrote the following:

". . . After True Health, Inc.'s announcement July 16, serious questions have arisen about the validity of the company's research and the legal and ethical issues of selling desperate AIDS patients an expensive treatment that may have no therapeutic value."

Jacobson quoted FDA media spokesman Brad Stone, who said:

"We're always concerned about anything that might be an unproven medical claim. By virtue of the company's announcement that its product has therapeutic effect, it comes under our jurisdiction."

Before the start of the AIDS test, Dr. Pulse had contacted Douglas Dillon of the Food and Drug Administration in Washington D.C. Dillon told Pulse that the FDA did not need to be involved with True Health's AIDS test since the products to be used were classified as nutritional. After the astounding mid-point results, Dr. Pulse outlined in a letter to the FDA the medical data from the test and asked the FDA to provide "federal guidance at this juncture in the global war on AIDS." Dr. Pulse relayed this information at the press conference, but Jacobson didn't bother to report it.

Both Stokley and Dr. Pulse had emphasized to reporters that further research was necessary, that they had and were still requesting FDA involvement in the study. Dr. Pulse also acknowledged that the test fell short of the requirements of meticulous FDA guidelines mainly because of the urgency of the AIDS epidemic. Indeed, the FDA had recently shortened the traditional process for reviewing new AIDS drugs for that very reason. Choosing to ignore these facts, Jacobson quoted Dr. Daniel Barbaro, former director of the AIDS clinic at Parkland Memorial Hospital, who had not even attended the press conference. Barbaro maintained it would be difficult to determine the effectiveness of True Health's nutritional treatment based on the study: "It appears to have been a fairly healthy group of patients to begin with." Jacobson knew this statement was false, having heard Dr. Pulse describe the condition of the patients at the news conference:

"We had Walter Reed Scores as high as 12. Patients were literally on the brink of death. One was carried in, another came in a wheel chair, others were sheltered with people on either side of them. I'm not talking about a Lazarus phenomenon, where they were dead, literally. But their immune systems were dead, and in others, they looked good physically but their immune systems were shot. Sixteen had AIDS when they came into the study, twelve had ARC, and the rest were seropositive."

Dr. Barbaro had not discussed the test results with Dr. Pulse, met with any of the patients, or reviewed the statistical analysis of the AIDS test, yet Sherry Jacobson chose to report his perceptions regarding the validity of True Health's clinical trial. At no time did she interview Stokley, Dr. Pulse, or anyone affiliated with True Health to confirm the accuracy of her article.

A few weeks later, Jacobson further disparaged True Health in the *Dallas Morning News*, intimating that True Health deliberately did not involve the FDA in their trial and that test patients were paying for their treatment. She interviewed Ken Davis, Chief of Drug Investigations in Texas' Department of Health—Division of Food & Drugs, who said his office was "concerned about the safety and efficacy of the product and whether people were being 'ripped off'." She also talked to FDA spokesman Brad Stone again, who maintained that True Health would have to apply for an Investigational New Drug (IND) claim before proceeding with their test, and that the FDA had "an understanding with True Health that there will be no further promotional activities for the treatment until studies are done under our [FDA] sanction." Finally, in an obvious attempt to destroy Dr. Pulse's credibility, Jacobson challenged his personal and professional ethics.

The reporter from the *Dallas Morning News* did not include *the facts* in her article: that the Investigational Review Board at Dallas-Fort Worth Medical Center had reviewed Dr. Pulse's findings; that Southern Methodist University ran statistical norms on all test data, confirming Walter Reed and Karnofsky statistics; and that all lab tests were performed at Damon Clinical Laboratories.

Stokley was shocked and outraged by the lack of response and erroneous reporting of the media. The only other newspaper to cover True Health's AIDS test, the *Wichita Falls Times Record*, reported True Health's outrage at their treatment by the media. Misrepresented by the *Dallas Morning News*, which proved to be a reliable outlet for FDA propaganda, and stonewalled by the government, Stokley felt True Health's problems stemmed from the medical establishment's bias toward toxic drugs to treat AIDS and other diseases, as opposed to using nutrition to boost the body's own ability to fight illness.

True Health sent videotapes of the press conference to the networks—CNN, ABC, NBC, and CBS, and to *Newsweek* and *Time*, and not one of these powerful institutions acknowledged receiving the tapes. An advertising executive in New York City told True Health's media director that "the networks wouldn't 'touch' True Health" because they were too afraid of losing advertising money from the pharmaceutical industry. Channel 5 was the only television station in Dallas to air information on the AIDS test, and their broadcast was similar in tone to that of the *Dallas Morning News*—compressed, derogatory, and riddled with inaccuracies and misconceptions.

Paul D. Bailey, Chairman of the AIDS Recovery Foundation in Dallas, wrote to Stokley:

"We have been astonished by the results of the study involving your nutritional product . . . It saddens us to see the slow and somewhat skeptical response on the part of the media to the announcement of these remarkable test results and their implications, but we know that they will eventually turn around. Then you will not be able to keep them out of your front door! Our organization's Board of Directors unanimously voted to offer your nutritional supplement to those individuals afflicted with AIDS, as we believe it will be the treatment of choice over other products currently in use."

Ten days after the press conference, Stokley wrote a letter to President Bush:

". . . Due to the astounding nature of the test results presented at the press conference, we expected the information presented to be treated with a certain amount of incredulity. We were also prepared for the fact that the ensuing news coverage might be somewhat delayed as the media performed the necessary research to write their stories . . . We have been in contact with Sharon Fitzpatrick, who is establishing the National AIDS Task Force at the request of your office, and have sent her a complete media kit including a press release and videotape. Dr. Pulse also contacted the FDA on more than one occasion to advise them of the study and its ongoing progress, despite reports to the contrary . . . We take a strong objection to the media setting itself up, not only as the conscience, but also the God-given mind of the individuals of this great nation. The press is using its power to effectively censor this information which should, by rights, be impartially reported so that each American can freely, as is their constitutional right, make their own personal decision on the matter. We have nothing to hide. We invite any responsible inquiry about our company, its formulation and this study which has produced such astounding results. We only ask that the inquiry and research result in a truthful and fair reporting to the people of America and the world . . . We are asking for whatever assistance your office can provide us in seeking to remedy this gross abuse of the power of the press. Lives are at stake and the clock is ticking. We ask only for fairness, and for our right as Americans to be heard. It is a matter of life and death for many."

Copies of this letter were sent to the *Dallas Morning News*, Channel 5 in Dallas, Dr. Daniel Barbaro, the Texas Department of Health, President Bush, Senator Lloyd Bentson and Senator Phil Gramm.

This was Stokley's first experience with the manipulated news story, where the news is fed to us along certain lines that have already been decided, where the establishment media is none other than an instrument for government propaganda. Big Brother is alive and well, as George Orwell's creation has become a frightening reality.

CHAPTER FIVE

INNOCENT CASUALTIES IN A WAR

Thou majestic in thy sadness
At the doubtful doom of human kind.

Tennyson

A few weeks after the press conference, FDA agents Joel Martinez and Ken Davis visited True Health's corporate offices. Despite his previous dealings with the FDA, Stokley assumed the agents had come to congratulate True Health, and that after examining the materials True Health had sent them—a videotape of the press conference and documentation confirming the test results—the FDA would provide federal assistance at this critical juncture.

Yet instead of wanting to expand on valuable research that warranted further investigation, the Food and Drug Administration was prepared to do everything in its power to shut True Health down. The agents presented Stokley with a Notice of Investigation: Martinez, an investigator with the Dallas FDA, led the formal questioning, while Davis, an FDA official with the Texas Department of Health (who had criticized True Health in the *Dallas Morning News*), chimed in on occasion. Robert Williams, Vice President of True Health, was in the room with Stokley during the entire interrogation.

Stokley reminded the agents that True Health had already sent the FDA a videotape and press kit describing the AIDS test. He told them he did not want the FDA as adversaries, that he needed their support in order to make a final determination on the validity of True Health's AIDS test. "Anything you want or need, just ask us and we will provide it for you," Stokley repeated several times during the agents' visit. He explained that although True Health undertook the AIDS study because previous clinical AIDS trials had not involved nutrition, they had not expected a showing of such magnitude.

At first the FDA officials insisted that True Health's nutritional study had been released too soon; they also expressed concern over the amount of money True Health was charging test patients for the product. Stokley told them it was being supplied free of cost, as were the medical tests and Dr. Pulse's services. Whereupon the investigators decided that the nutritional supplement should be classified as a drug since it was a possible "cure" for AIDS. Ken Davis asked Stokley if he wanted to proceed with a drug classification, but Stokley immediately declined. To designate True Health's nutritional product a drug would be as ludicrous as writing a prescription for Vitamin C. Moreover, it takes about twelve years and $231 million to go to from the synthesis to the approval of a new drug.[7] AIDS patients could not wait twelve years for the government to approve a non-toxic nutritional supplement. Even if Stokley had wanted to have True Health's product classified as a drug, his small company could never have afforded the exorbitant funds.

Stokley presented the agents with True Health's test results, and requested, once again, the FDA's assistance so that they could "begin saving lives." Ken Davis replied that whatever worked was fine with him—he didn't care if True Health used peanut hulls in its product.

Davis was determined to talk Stokley into classifying the nutritional supplement as a drug; he even claimed that a couple of items in True Health's supplement could cause the product to be *designated* as a drug. When Stokley continued to resist, Davis retreated to his original contention, that thirty patients were not enough to consider True Health's test a "good study." Exasperated, Stokley explained how the patients' overall conditions had improved, and that Dr. Pulse believed ten of the patients would be dead by now if they had not been taking the product.

After scanning a list of all the ingredients in True Health's product, Inspector Davis spotted an unlabeled bottle of aloe vera and said it would have to be embargoed, ostensibly because it wasn't properly licensed by the State of Texas. Stokley offered to set aside the aloe until it was properly labeled, but Davis insisted the embargoed aloe would have to be destroyed. He offered to send Stokley a licensing application

---

[7] See Appendix D for New Drug Application procedures.

for future use. Stokley protested—in his previous experiences with the FDA, it took months to get anything done. The aloe vera was only being used in the test; it was not being sold. He was concerned that the balance of the 180-day test might be interrupted. The FDA officers laughed, saying it wasn't their problem. Determined to obstruct True Health's AIDS test, the agents detained 283 quart bottles of aloe vera juice for six months, until 2 February 1990.

A few days later, Joel Martinez inspected Dr. Pulse's clinic in Grand Prairie, Texas. As he browsed through AIDS test patients' files, he told Dr. Pulse and his assistant, Elizabeth Uhlig: "It is against God's law to save those gays." Martinez later repeated the exact same statement to Stokley. Trying to appeal to an iota of decency that the inspector might have, Stokley asked him about the innocent children and adults who were contracting AIDS through blood transfusions. Our representative from the Food and Drug Administration shrugged: "In a war there are always innocent casualties."

Despite the embargo, True Health had enough aloe vera in storage to complete the 180-day test. The results at the completion of the AIDS test were just as spectacular as those at the mid-point. The Modified Walter Reed Scale shows improvement when it decreases: All twenty-nine of the patients had lower Walter Reed scores at 90 days for 100 percent improvement as a group; at 180 days two patients remained the same and twenty-seven improved further for 96.4 percent improvement.

According to the Karnofsky Quality of Life Assessment (which shows improvement when it increases), twenty-seven patients improved after 90 days and two remained the same for 93.1 percent improvement; all improved at 180 days for 100 percent improvement.

Of greatest significance at 180 days was the P24 core antigen assay, which is a measurement of *viral replication*: At 90 days three out of twelve patients had converted to *nonreactive*, and at 180 days this figure remained the same. At the beginning of the test, twelve patients had non-functioning immune systems. After 180 days of participating in the AIDS experiment, ten of these patients had regained their immune functions. Dr. Donald B. Owen of Southern Methodist University told Stokley this was "Nobel Prize work"—it was the first time immune systems had been "restarted."

Just what kind of response did the federal government give True Health's AIDS test? Stokley received several letters from various government departments, in answer to letters he had sent to President Bush, FDA Commissioner Frank Young, and Secretary of Health & Human Services Louis Sullivan. Sharon Fitzpatrick, Deputy Associate Director of Presidential Personnel, replied for President Bush: "I have forwarded AIDS test materials to James R. Allen, Director of National

AIDS Program Office." Hugh C. Cannon, Associate Commissioner for Legislative Affairs, also wrote to Stokley: "We have asked the appropriate officials in the Agency (Department of Health & Human Services) for their review. You will be hearing from them directly." Cannon sent a carbon copy of this letter to White House assistant Sally Kelley.

At the FDA, Ellen Cooper, M.D., wrote a letter for Frank Young, confirming receipt of Dr. Pulse's letter to Young about the AIDS test, as well as a phone call between Dr. Pulse and Dr. Paul Beninger (FDA). Dr. Cooper enclosed in the letter a pre-IND guidance form for development of anti-HIV drug products, and suggested that Dr. Pulse contact preclinical supervisors listed in the letter. Dr. Cooper added that information on True Health's AIDS test had been forwarded to the NIH's AIDS Clinical Drug Development Committee (ACDDC).

It was on the record—the White House, the Department of Health & Human Services, and the FDA had acknowledged in writing that they had received Stokley's and Dr. Pulse's letters regarding True Health's AIDS test. What they would do remained to be seen.

In the meantime, FDA agent Harold Davis had an offer for Stokley: "If you'll give me the formula, I'll fix it so you can sell this product as a nutritional thing." Stokley sent him the formula, but not the source—it is impossible to duplicate True Health's nutritional supplement without knowing the source of the ingredients. Stokley maintains that Davis never "fixed it" because he could not copy True Health's formula. Instead, Stokley received a letter from the FDA's Center for Food Safety & Applied Nutrition that criticized True Health's labeling.

A year went by and Stokley had still not heard anything positive from the federal government. He was given the bureaucratic runaround: form letters telling him to write to one department, then to another department and another—it was endless.

On 14 June 1990 Stokley wrote to Secretary Louis Sullivan:

". . . We spent over $200,000 doing this test. I feel it is a terrible injustice to people who have AIDS, to have a product like this available, which is totally non-toxic, with no side effects . . . and yet, no one is interested enough to even look at the test results."

Lawrence Deyton, M.D., of the National Institutes of Allergies and Infectious Disease (NIAID) Division of AIDS, responded on behalf of Secretary Sullivan:

". . . The AIDS Clinical Drug Development Committee reviewed data provided in support of studying acemannan, an active ingredient of aloe vera leaves, at its October 1988 and May 1990 meetings. Based on data submitted by True Health, the committee recommended that acemannan [aloe vera] not be studied further in federally-funded clinical trials . . . NS2 was conducted to investigate only the nutritional supplement and fatty acid capsules. The results reportedly were similar to those obtained when aloe vera juice was included. Either of these treatment approaches might be of interest for further testing to clinicians within the CPCRA who may share your clinical and research interests."

Might be of interest for further testing? Dr. Anthony Fauci, Director of NIAID, had been given the responsibility to run the federal government's AIDS program, to conduct all of the federally-funded clinical AIDS trials, and NIAID refused to test True Health's nutritional supplement in a government sponsored trial. There had not been a federal clinical AIDS trial that had come close to the success that True Health experienced, not to mention a treatment without detrimental side effects. And the United States government repudiated it.

CHAPTER SIX

FTC vs. INTERNATIONAL WHITE CROSS

A test or study shall be considered competent and reliable if the United States Food and Drug Administration has accepted it as the basis for approving said drug as a treatment for HIV-disease.

U.S. District Court
Northern California, 1991

Although the federal government refused to acknowledge the extraordinary results of True Health's AIDS test, advertising executive Alan Weiss did not. Weiss contacted Stokley to inquire about the possibility of True Health selling its product to an Indian tribe in Hopland, California, where AIDS was rampant due to extensive drug use.

Stokley authorized the sale of the nutritional supplement, and the Hopland Indians marketed True Health's product under the name "Immune Plus." The Hopland Indians produced their own labels and called themselves the International White Cross. Dan and Judith Gagliardo handled the business transactions between International White Cross and True Health, and Alan Weiss' agency, AMW Advertising, created the advertisements.

On 12 November 1990 an Immune Plus ad appeared in the *San Francisco Chronicle*:

> "AMAZING RESULTS
> IMPROVE
> IMMUNE SYSTEMS!
> This is for ANYONE suffering from AIDS,
> exposed to the HIV Virus, or just
> concerned about staying healthy.
> LOOK AT THESE DRAMATIC REAL LIFE TEST RESULTS!
> 180 DAY TEST SHOWS IMMUNE SYSTEMS REACTIVATED
> *THIS IS NOT A DRUG

> These results were from a combination of products, including a balanced vitamin, mineral and protein formula and essential fatty acid capsules, now offered through Immune + PLUS. The products have shown efficacy and safety. According to VITAMIN MAGAZINE, "The rapid mutation of the HIV virus will, in all likelihood, preclude the possibility of perfecting a vaccine for this dreaded disease in the near future. THE RESULTS OF THIS AIDS TREATMENT STUDY ARE TRULY EXCITING, AND A STRONG INDICATION THAT STRENGTHENING THE BODY'S NATURAL IMMUNE SYSTEM MAY PROVE TO BE THE SINGLE MOST POWERFUL WEAPON IN THE WAR AGAINST AIDS."

Within a few days after this ad first appeared in the *San Francisco Chronicle*, the Federal Trade Commission (FTC) was alerted. The FTC files a complaint when it has "reason to believe" the law is being violated and that a proceeding is in "the public interest." Alleging that false claims had been made, the FTC launched an investigation and lawsuit against True Health, International White Cross, and Alan M. Weiss.[8] With assistance from FDA offices in Dallas and San Francisco, the California Food and Agriculture Department, the Texas Department of Health, and offices of the Attorneys General of California and Texas, the FTC obtained a temporary restraining order and a preliminary injunction halting the sale and advertising of Immune Plus and requested a redress for consumers. Certainly, the FTC was acting under the aus-

---

[8] See Appendix E for FTC Court Order Requesting Permanent Injunction.

pices of the FDA: By making True Health the target of another government agency, the FDA could destroy True Health financially.

Charging that Immune Plus was useless as a "cure" for AIDS, the FTC indicted True Health on the front page of its newspaper, *FTC News*. In the article, "FTC Charges Producers and Marketers of 'Immune Plus' with Making False Claims About Its Ability to Cure Aids," the FTC accused the producers and marketers of Immune Plus with false advertising and deceptive marketing. According to the FTC, defendants (True Health, International White Cross, and Alan Weiss) represented Immune Plus as a cure for patients with AIDS or ARC, causing them to go into remission or to become HIV-negative. Defendants' practices caused "substantial financial injury" to consumers and also may have led individuals in need of other treatments to forego them.

*Of the four people who had a chance to purchase Immune Plus before the court injunction, three of them posed as interested buyers at the request of the FTC: The FDA arranged for FDA inspector Kenneth O'Kihara and FDA investigator Paul Walfoort to call the ad's 800 number and order Immune Plus, while the FTC asked Dr. John Renner, President of Consumer's Health Information and Research Institute, to place the third false order. How could the FTC possibly know whether Immune Plus worked when the people who bought the product—the people they had **set-up**—were not even sick? Only one of the four people who bought the product could have been ill, and in all likelihood, that person was under some kind of medical treatment.*

In the years since Stokley took control, True Health had not received one complaint about their nutritional supplement, nor had International White Cross in its few days of operation. It was obvious that the FTC was not interested in whether Immune Plus helped in the treatment of AIDS; they were only interested in curtailing its marketing.

The FTC alleged that Immune Plus was being advertised as a "cure" for AIDS. At no time did True Health or International White Cross claim to have a cure. Test results in the Immune Plus ad were taken directly from the nutritional AIDS test, and True Health sold the exact same formula that was used in their AIDS test to International White Cross. Immune Plus was not a drug; it was a balanced vitamin, mineral, and protein supplement taken in conjunction with essential fatty acid capsules. The ad for Immune Plus explicitly said, "This is not a drug."

On 20 December 1990 Sandy Zeigler, an FDA investigator with the Dallas office, and Thomas Brinck, an FDA investigator with the Texas Department of Health, served Stokley with an official notice requesting to review and copy distribution records for all foods and drugs distributed, manufactured, packed, or held by True Health from 1988 through 1990. Stokley immediately informed them that he was videotaping the entire conversation—"I'll make copies for you if you want"—and that True Health was operating under the Ninth Amendment. Article IX of the U.S. Constitution states that freedom of choice in medicine and health care is a right retained by the people under the Ninth Amendment.[9]

Stokley:

"I'll tell you what I'm looking at . . . We've made all our information available for the FDA. We've requested help, support. We talked to them about an IND—we've received nothing. We don't even get a response, and some of the things that have gone on haven't been legal . . . We always end up with a different person, and I'm tired of it. I just keep gathering material and sending it over [to the FDA] . . . I made an agreement with Mr. Davis in Washington D.C. I agreed to release our formula and all our data to the FDA; in turn, the FDA agreed to give me a letter to go forward and make our own nutritional product and sell it as a nutritional product. That agreement was made and I went back to them and I can't get them to keep the agreement . . . We've tried to work with the people in Washington D.C.; we've tried and can't work with them. There's no way we can communicate with them. Other fellahs like you come in here, they give us their advice, we follow it and we still get nowhere."

Zeigler:

"I'm a Senior Investigator . . . It's very hard for me to believe that you asked for an IND and didn't receive it."

Stokley:

"I can tell you the date—September 8, 1989. We accepted Davis' proposal . . . We gave all that information to the FDA about our test, and when the newspapers called them, they said they never heard of us, and, boy, that made me mad. I called that Brad Stone up, your PR man in Washington, D.C. We furnished all that stuff way before the study was released. We made copies of it available to everyone. We sent it to the National Institutes of Health, to Dr. Fauci, to Dr. Young, to a Dr. Mason who was the Assistant to Dr. Young . . . We were trying to be as cooperative as we could

---

[9] See Appendix F for Ninth Amendment Arguments.

be. We sent copies to the Texas Health Department, to ABC, NBC, CBS. It's all out there, you just haven't seen it."

Conscious of the videotape running, Zeigler and Brinck said little in response. After Stokley gave them a quick tour of the facilities, the two men departed.

As if the FTC lawsuit wasn't enough, the Texas Department of Health joined in the act—at the urging of the FDA, no doubt. On 7 January 1991 the Austin-based office charged True Health with "deceptive trade practice in violation of the Texas Deceptive Trade Practices and Consumer Protection Act." In a letter to Stokley's attorney, Oscar "Buddy" W. Loyd, Texas Assistant Attorney General Robert Reyna proposed the following "Agreed Final Judgment and Permanent Injunction":

"... I have determined that the minimum amount for which this case can be settled is $10,000. I know that you informed me that your client is short of funds. The advantage to him in settling his involvement with these products at this time is that he would face no further liability to the State in future litigation over this matter. As you know, this investigation is continuing. Mr. Stokley's involvement with the marketing of his formulas as an AIDS preventative or cure is still as of now a subject of investigation."

The press continued to espouse the government line. In a 9 February 1991 article in the *Sacramento Bee Final*, reporter Clair Cooper quoted FTC attorney David Newman as claiming that Immune Plus was being heavily promoted in Northern California, especially in the San Francisco area, to appeal to the gay community. Larry Tate of Project Inform, a San Francisco-based AIDS information hotline, told Cooper that knowledge of the FTC lawsuit induced his organization to discontinue advertisements for Immune Plus. Cooper did not bother to interview True Health, International White Cross, or Alan Weiss for their side of the story.

On 12 February 1991 Stokley was served with an FTC notice requiring his presence at a preliminary San Francisco Court hearing; he received the notice just two days before the date of the hearing. Obviously intentional, the FTC failed to notify the parties named in the lawsuit in advance, leaving them no time for logistics, communication needs, proper legal evaluation, or travel arrangements.

Two and a half months later, another hearing took place in San Francisco—in the Judge's Chamber—to determine whether the FTC had enough of a case to warrant a trial by jury. Stokley was the only defendant to attend in person; he wanted to ensure that True Health received due process. The Gagliardos (representing International White Cross) and Alan Weiss chose to send the court written statements.

The FTC engaged Dr. Daniel Barbaro (who had criticized True Health in the *Dallas Morning News*) to testify on their behalf. In a written statement, Barbaro claimed:

"Some of my HIV disease patients take nutritional supplements. I have seen no difference in the course of HIV disease between those persons taking nutritional supplements and those who did not."

Apparently, Barbaro and the FTC did not consider it significant that Barbaro had never used True Health's product.

The FTC arranged for another medical doctor, Carl Grunfeld, with the Veterans Affairs Medical Center in San Francisco, to testify on their behalf. Dr. Grunfeld maintained that HIV disease had "no clear-cut relationship between the intake of nutrients and HIV disease." In the most successful nutritional treatment for AIDS he had seen, some patients gained weight and felt better, but there was no increase in T-4 cell counts: "HIV is clearly more than advanced malnutrition . . . My opinion is that the Pulse study is totally meaningless." Like Barbaro, Grunfeld was not familiar with True Health's product. In fact, none of the witnesses testifying on the FTC's behalf had any first-hand experience with *True Health*; they were judging it by other products' standards.

Paul Volberding, M.D., another witness for the FTC, tried to discredit Dr. Pulse's credentials by saying he had never been published. This was false, as Dr. Pulse's article on the 180-day AIDS test had been published the previous winter in the *Journal of Advancement in Medicine*. Stokley had made available to the court the article, which was entitled, "A Significant Improvement in a Clinical Pilot Study Utilizing Nutritional Supplements, Essential Fatty Acids and Stabilized Aloe Vera Juice in 29 HIV Seropositive, ARC and AIDS Patients." The board of directors of the journal obviously considered Dr. Pulse and True Health credible.

Stokley considered the hearing a sham. When it was finally his turn to speak, he recounted True Health's AIDS test in detail, described the amazing results, and even suggested that True Health's test patients appear before the court in person, to demonstrate the validity of test results.

The final outcome of the hearing was a real travesty: The U.S. District Court of Northern California gave the FDA complete authority to decide whether a test would be considered "competent and reliable" as the basis for an AIDS treatment. As a consequence, True Health was prohibited from advocating its nutritional supplement as a treatment for AIDS.

In the "Final Settlement," True Health was ordered by the court to restrain from making or assisting others in making, directly or by implication, any oral or written statement or representation that:

"The use of Immune Plus or any product containing the same or substantially similar formulation will cure HIV-disease;

The use of Immune Plus or any product containing the same or substantially similar formulation will cause HIV-disease to go into remission;

The use of Immune Plus or any product containing the same or substantially similar formulation will cause persons who have tested as HIV-positive to become HIV-negative;

The use of Immune Plus or any product containing the same or substantially similar formulation will eliminate or alleviate the symptoms of HIV-disease; or

The efficacy of Immune Plus or any product containing the same or substantially similar formulation in the treatment of HIV-disease has been demonstrated by scientifically valid clinical studies."

The FDA was still in control—so much for justice. True Health was forced to refrain from selling or giving their product to AIDS patients as a treatment for AIDS, to stop giving the product out as they had been, free of charge, to the patients who had participated in the test. And because AIDS patients were afraid of FDA harassment, many of them stopped taking *True Health*—they feared negative publicity (or any publicity at all) concerning their predicament; they had observed, first-hand, the *Dallas Morning News'* attempt to destroy Dr. Pulse's credibility. FDA agents had threatened Stokley, Dr. Pulse, and Elizabeth Uhlig that the FDA would seize UPS statements in order to have access to the names and addresses of *all* True Health customers.

Stokley would have preferred to continue giving the product to AIDS patients, but he simply could not risk government entrapment. Everything within him wanted to fight the federal government, to challenge the FDA in court. However, between the cost of the AIDS test and the decrease in True Health sales which resulted from the government's harassment, he was financially drained—exactly what the FDA had intended. *Small businesses are a common target for the FDA because they do not have the funds or political lobbying power to fight back.* It is interesting to note that subsequent to the San Francisco hearing, the Texas Department of Health stopped harassing True Health, despite Stokley's refusal to pay the $10,000 "fine."

Attorney Jay Geller, an authority on FDA law and former employee in the general counsel's office of the FDA, observed: "The FDA has very wide-ranging regulatory powers that are restricted only by the courts. However, the FDA is rarely restricted by the courts because it is considered to be an agency of experts dealing with expert issues."

Marion Moss, a former investigator with the Texas Attorney General's office, commented in 1992: "During the eight years I was an investigator with the Texas Attorney General's office, I had numerous occasions to work with the FDA on cases involving potential health fraud. I repeatedly saw cases against large corporations . . . go unchallenged . . . Instead, the agency chose [to pursue] cases against alternative health care providers and minor companies . . ."

In the final analysis, True Health was offering a nutritional support that would hopefully improve the quality and lengthen the lives of AIDS patients. A few months after the court order, True Health Vice President Robert Williams lamented:

"AIDS patients are calling in all the time wanting the product, but we haven't sold it yet. That's tragic, because with the results we've seen, it's hard not to let the people who need it have it."

We have been indoctrinated with the ideology that the law is ours. The truth is that the federal government is not a neutral force reflecting competing interests: When the government decides to go after someone, it uses every arsenal of power—the FDA, the FTC, the IRS. Government litigation drags on and on since its funds—taxpayers' money—are endless. As long as the FDA is allowed to use its police powers to harass and destroy free market competitors, the law will be nothing more than the "interests of the stronger."

Richard Stokley, President of True Health

56

Pam Chaplin, who suffers from multiple sclerosis, has not had an attack since she started taking True Health's nutritional supplement five years ago. The photo on the top was taken before Pam discovered *True Health*. The photo on the bottom was taken recently.

Immediately after undergoing a kidney transplant, Lennie Meyers supplemented his anti-rejection medication with *True Health*. He has not experienced a rejection episode in the eight years since the transplant.

November 28, 1988

Congressman Jim Wright
Congress of the United States
House of Representatives
Office of the Speaker
Washington, DC 20515

Dear Congressman Wright,

I appreciate your help in the matter concerning the
FDA and Evening Primrose Oil and gamma linolenic acid.

I am writing this letter to let you know that we
are having assembled papers and studies to answer the
specific charges that the FDA has against these products.

I believe we will have everything ready in about
ten days and I will contact you then to move forward.

Thank you again for your help.

Sincerely yours,

TRUE HEALTH, INC.

Richard M. Stokley
CEO

RMS/am

P.O. BOX 38664   DALLAS, TEXAS 75238   214·644·1200

After the FDA seized and destroyed $24,000 worth of True Health's
essential fatty acid capsules, Speaker of the House Jim Wright contacted
the FDA on True Health's behalf.

Journal of Advancement in Medicine
Volume 3, Number 4, Winter 1990

A Significant Improvement in a Clinical Pilot Study Utilizing Nutritional Supplements, Essential Fatty Acids and Stabilized Aloe Vera Juice in 29 HIV Seropositive, ARC and AIDS Patients

T. L. Pulse, M.D. and Elizabeth Uhlig, RRA

ABSTRACT: It has been found that poor nutrition is one of the risk factors for progressing from HIV seropositive into ARC and into AIDS. By improving the patient's nutritional status the possibility of progressing into AIDS Related Complex (ARC) or Acquired Immune Deficiency Syndrome (AIDS) may be reduced or at least delayed, and the goal is to place the patient into long term remission.[1] To attempt to accomplish this end, a powdered nutritional supplementation was provided to study participants together with essential fatty acids and stabilized 100% pure Aloe Vera Juice for a study period of 180 days.[2] At the conclusion of the study, the participants had improved both clinically and functionally. Most patients who were symptomatic reported that within three to five days their symptoms had subsided and they had gained weight. This regimen of nutritional supplementation is cost effective and non-toxic and can be an important factor in halting the progression of the HIV virus by boosting the immune system, decreasing the P24 core antigen activity and improving the overall quality of the patient's life.

Introduction

The possible beneficial effects of a balanced nutritional supplementation,[3-5] including essential fatty acids (EFA)[6-9] and Aloe Vera Juice in

---

Terry L. Pulse, M.D. is a family practice physician in general practice, who has been conducting ongoing AIDS research for the last three years. Address correspondence to Terry L. Pulse, M.D., 2701 Osler Dr., St. 2, Grand Prairie, TX 75051; tel: 214-660-1472.
Elizabeth Uhlig RRA is a research biologist with a background in medical record administration.

In its Winter 1990 issue, the *Journal of Advancement in Medicine* published an article on True Health's successful 180-day AIDS clinical trial.

July 25, 1989

Dear Mr. Stokley:

Thank you for forwarding the information and research regarding the nutritional AIDS TEST. True Health, Inc. discoveries on this most important epidemic facing our Nation are quite encouraging. I have taken the liberty of forwarding your information to those in the National AIDS Program office at the Department of Health and Human Services, as they are in the best position to review your findings. Your materials have been directly forwarded to:

> James R. Allen
> Director
> National AIDS Program Office
> Dept. of Health & Human Services
> 200 Independence Ave., S.W.
> Rm. 738 G - Humphrey Building
> Washington, D.C. 20201

I encourage you to contact their office in the future should you have additional information to provide. Thank you again, and I wish you great success with your program.

> Sincerely,
>
> *Sharon Fitzpatrick*
>
> Sharon Fitzpatrick
> Deputy Associate Director
> of Presidential Personnel

Mr. Richard M. Stokley
True Health, Inc.
P.O. Box 38664
Dallas, TX 75238

Both the White House and the Department of Health & Human Services responded to Stokley's letters regarding True Health's AIDS clinical trial.

DEPARTMENT OF HEALTH & HUMAN SERVICES   Public Health Service

National Institutes of Health
National Institute of Allergy
and Infectious Diseases
Bethesda, Maryland 20892

July 26, 1990

Mr. Richard M. Stokley
President
True Health, Inc.
P.O. Box 38664
Dallas, Texas 75238

Dear Mr. Stokley:

I am responding to your letter of June 14 to Dr. Louis W. Sullivan, Secretary,
Department of Health and Human Services, concerning a treatment for AIDS.
Because the National Institute of Allergy and Infectious Diseases (NIAID), a
component of the National Institutes of Health, has the major responsibility
in the Federal Government for basic and clinical research on AIDS, your letter
was referred to my office for reply.

The NIAID Division of Acquired Immunodeficiency Syndrome is very much involved
in the development of therapies for AIDS and has, in its Treatment Research
Branch, a mechanism for the review and evaluation of candidate therapies. The
NIAID keeps an open mind with respect to all of the suggestions received
regarding treatments and cures for AIDS and gives them due consideration.
They are reviewed for scientific merit and determinations are made on an
individual basis regarding where they belong within established priorities for
future studies.

To pursue your suggestion further, you should send a more complete description
of the proposed therapy for AIDS to:

> Dr. Jane Kinsel, Executive Secretary
> AIDS Clinical Drug Development Committee
> Treatment Research Branch, Division of AIDS
> National Institute of Allergy and Infectious Diseases
> 6003 Executive Blvd., Room 202P
> Bethesda, MD 20892

I have been told that, in view of the very large volume of materials being
reviewed by this committee, you will be contacted only if there is some level
of interest or if additional information is required.

Thank you for your interest and for bringing this to our attention.

> Sincerely yours,
>
> Diane Shartsis Wax
> Planning Officer
> National Institute of Allergy
>   and Infectious Diseases

cc: Dr. Kinsel

HOUSE OF COMMONS

Third Report from the

SOCIAL SERVICES COMMITTEE

Session 1986-87

PROBLEMS ASSOCIATED WITH AIDS

Volume III
Minutes of Evidence (8 April - 13 May 1987) and Memoranda

Ordered by The House of Commons *to be printed*
13 May 1987

LONDON
HER MAJESTY'S STATIONERY OFFICE
£ 13.60 net

A 1987 British House of Commons report on AIDS delineated the "scale of deception and misinformation" perpetrated by virologists, clinicians, journalists, and politicians.

PART II

CHAPTER SEVEN

THE FDA—AS DANGEROUS AS THE WORST DISEASE

The thing that bugs me is that the people think the FDA is protecting them. It isn't. What the FDA is doing and what the public thinks it's doing are as different as night and day.

Dr. Herbert Ley
Former FDA Commissioner

The Food and Drug Administration is unrelenting in its war on organic vitamins, food supplements—anything that isn't classified as a drug. Although there are many natural treatments for a variety of ailments, such as arthritis and heart disease, that have been tested and proven effective and safe, the FDA tries to keep them off the market. The most basic weapons in the fight against disease—nutrients that keep the cells in our bodies healthy—have been in danger of being banned or legislated into prescriptions drugs. At the same time, the FDA has shown an astonishing lack of concern when it comes to the dangers of prescription drugs.

CREATION OF THE FDA

The Pure Food and Drug Act of 1906 created the FDA, giving the regulatory agency broad powers over the food and drug industries. As a branch of the Department of Health & Human Services, the FDA is funded by Congress and has the authority to regulate foods, drugs, cosmetics, and medical devices that are sold within the U.S. including those that are imported. The FDA has wide-ranging regulatory powers, such as pre-marketing approval of drugs, medical devices, food additives and food coloring, as well as jurisdiction over products shipped across state lines. It is the FDA's responsibility to ensure that products are pure and unadulterated and not misrepresented by erroneous labeling.

Until 1938 drugs did not have to be shown to be either safe or effective. However after 107 Americans died from the "wonder drug" sulfanilamide, President Roosevelt signed legislation that authorized the FDA to prevent the marketing of a drug product unless it could be shown to be *safe*. Then, in 1962, the thalidomide tragedy occurred: 10,000 babies in foreign countries were born deformed as a result of pregnant women's intake of the German-developed tranquilizer. Thalidomide had never been approved for use in the U.S.[10] Nevertheless, Congress responded to the thalidomide catastrophe by approving the 1962 Kefauver-Harris amendments to the Food and Drug Act, which determined that drugs in the U.S. had to be shown to be *effective* as well as safe. The FDA obtained new, arbitrary powers—powers that they would abuse in their stringent regulation of vitamins and minerals.

HISTORY OF FDA EFFORTS TO RESTRICT DIETARY SUPPLEMENTS

In 1962 the FDA (with encouragement from the AMA) published regulations setting minimum and maximum levels for dietary supplements—an enraged citizen protest resulted in the withdrawal of these directives. Between 1966 and 1973, the FDA proposed new dietary legislation which would have allowed them to regulate most vitamins and minerals as drugs: Vitamins that exceeded 150 percent of the RDA would have been classified as over-the-counter drugs; Vitamins A and D, and Vitamin C in excess of 90 milligrams would have been designated prescription drugs; combinations of vitamins and minerals would have been prohibited.

---

[10] The FDA has recently sanctioned clinical trials of thalidomide as an AIDS treatment.

Congress received more mail against the FDA's vitamin proposals than on any other issue except Watergate and Vietnam. Urged on by angry constituents, Congress responded in 1976 by unanimously approving the Proxmire/Rogers Amendment to the Federal Food, Drug and Cosmetic Act. The Proxmire Amendment prohibited the FDA from regulating vitamins as prescription drugs. According to Senator Proxmire:

"The FDA and much, but not all, of the orthodox medical profession are actively hostile against the manufacture, sale, and distribution of vitamins and minerals as food or food supplements. They are out to get the health food industry and to drive the health food stores out of business. And they are trying to do this out of active hostility and prejudice."

The 1976 Proxmire Amendment classified nutritional supplements as foods and gave consumers access to them at a reasonable cost. It was designed to prevent the FDA from limiting vitamin potencies, thus ensuring the consumer's right to purchase dietary supplements in the amount, combination, and potency desired.

THE FDA'S WAR ON "QUACKERY"

In the fall of 1971, the FDA also made a serious attempt to halt the growth of the increasingly popular field of alternative medicine. By defining all unorthodox medical treatments as "quackery," which they interpreted as "misinformation about health," the FDA attempted to prevent physicians, manufacturers, and consumers from practicing alternative therapies. The federal government's war against quackery was supported by the pharmaceutical companies and the AMA. In 1985 the Pharmaceutical Advertising Council and the FDA solicited funds from the pharmaceutical industry to combat medical quackery; they also issued a joint statement addressed to the presidents of advertising and PR agencies nationwide, asking them to cooperate with the anti-quackery campaign.[11]

The orthodox medical establishment wanted the public to become totally dependent on doctors and prescription drugs.

---

[11] This statement was written on joint letterhead from the FDA and the Pharmaceutical Advertising Council, and was signed by the directors of both organizations.

Nutritional experts were reluctant to defend their positions publicly due to fear of retribution by the FDA and AMA: Nutritionists were threatened with loss of grants and ruined reputations if they published positive results from nutritional tests. Their fears were not imagined. Two-time Nobel prize winner Linus Pauling lost the respect and gained the ridicule of mainstream medicine when he became an adamant supporter of Vitamin C. Alternative-minded physicians were (and still are) publicly derided by the medical establishment; some have even had their licenses revoked.[12]

For years the AMA engaged in an illegal boycott against chiropractors; an injunction against their boycott was finally affirmed by the U.S. Court of Appeals for the 7th Circuit on 7 February 1990.

FDA RAIDS OF VITAMINS AND NATURAL FOOD PRODUCTS

Despite the passage of the Proxmire Amendment, the FDA *continued* in its attempts to limit public access to dietary supplements by claiming they were either toxic, a dangerous food additive, or labeled with "unsubstantiated" therapeutic claims. During the 1980s and early 1990s, the FDA raided medical clinics, health food manufacturers and health food stores throughout the United States, seizing hundreds of natural food substances.

In the early 1990s, the FDA raided the following establishments: seventeen health food stores in Texas; a Utah-based herb company distributing evening primrose oil; a dietary supplement company in Oregon; a black-currant oil distributor in Illinois; the Life Extension Foundation in Florida; an alternative medical clinic in Kent, Washington; Nutricology in San Leandro; herbalists in northern and southern California; and many other small businesses throughout the country.

Across the state of Texas, the FDA confiscated such products as Vitamin C, aloe vera, and herbal teas—health food stores were being raided for Sleepytime Tea! When dozens of food supplements were seized in simultaneous raids on twelve Whole Foods Markets, Sun Harvest Farms, and Ye Seekers Horizon, the story was buried on the last page of the Sports Section of the *Dallas Morning News*. An inspection of Houston's Ye Seekers by the Texas Department of Health resulted in the

---

[12] Due to widespread citizen protest, North Carolina, Alaska, Washington, New York, and Oklahoma passed legislation in the 1990s to prevent state medical boards from revoking or denying licenses to health care providers who use "alternative" drugless therapies that are not recognized by mainstream medicine. [Citizens For Health Report, Vol 3:1, 1995, pp. 1,10.]

seizure of 250 products valued at $25,000. All of the products were detained because of health claims, or labels with the words "immune" or "diet"; none of the products were detained due to safety concerns. Joe Dixon, Supervisory Investigator for the Texas Health Department's FDA division, described these seizures as part of a national crackdown by the federal FDA on health food "quackery": "There's a nationwide push on health fraud claims, and the FDA's involved. I would pretty well say that, in the future, those products won't be on the shelves."

In its May 1992 *Dietary Supplements Task Force* report, the FDA wrote:

"The Task Force considered various issues in its deliberations, including how to ensure the safety of dietary supplements; how to limit the potential for fraud, i.e., disease
claims made on labels or through other means, e.g., magazine articles; [how to] **ensure that the existence of dietary
supplements on the market does not act as a disincentive
for drug development...**"

On 31 March 1993 Michael Taylor, Deputy Commissioner for Policy for the FDA, stated:

"From a scientific standpoint, the claimed benefits of
many of these products [amino acid and herbal products]
are better evaluated in pharmacological rather than nutritional terms. . . . **It is a simple fact that these products are
legally drugs and properly regulated as such.**"

David Adams, another FDA Deputy Commissioner for Policy, warned the Drug Information Association at its annual meeting in July of 1993:

"Pay careful attention to what is happening [with dietary
supplements] in the legislative arena . . . If these efforts are
successful, there could be a class of products to compete
with approved drugs that are subject to less regulation than
approved drugs . . . **the establishment of a separate regula-**

tory category for supplements could undercut exclusivity
rights enjoyed by holders of approved drug applications. "

In 1993 the FDA continued its efforts to restrict health claims,
raiding thirty-five health food facilities in seven states. Clearly, the FDA
is operating as the right arm of the pharmaceutical industry, for whom
natural remedies and treatments are a significant threat.

THE AMERICAN MEDICAL MONOPOLY

Most of the orthodox medical profession oppose the manufacture, sale, and distribution of vitamins and minerals as food or food supplements. Organizations helping to enforce this archaic system are the
FDA—whose employees are generally recruited from the medical and
pharmaceutical industries and law enforcement agencies; the
Department of Health & Human Services; state Departments of Health
(who work with the FDA); and the various medical foundations (such as
the American Cancer Society). In the name of "protecting the people" in
the field of nutrition, the medical establishment promotes misinformation. The result is that our health care services do not provide us with
optimum health care.[13]
We only have to look as far as the corporate structure of
America to understand why nutritional cures are not wanted. Vitamins
pose an enormous threat to the financial security of those with vested
interests. Consider all of the money spent on cancer, heart, and arthritis
research, and the hundreds of thousands of jobs provided. The
American medical monopoly has created a climate of scientific bias,
where there is an emphasis on drug research rather than nutrition
research. *Vitamins and herbs cannot be patented: As a consequence, the pharmaceutical industry is reluctant to invest research money on nutritional studies.*
Medical treatment in the U.S. is a commodity, and the monetary
stakes are enormous. In 1993 the American health care industry generat-
ed more than $942.5 billion in expenditures and employed more than 10
million people—2 million nurses, 650,000 doctors, and 150,000 dentists.
The industry supported 126 medical schools, approximately 6,600 hospi-

---

[13] See Appendix A —"The Benefits of Nutrition" —for detailed information
on the U.S. Health Care System and its antipathy towards nutrition.

tals, 1,100 health insurance companies and 25,600 nursing care facilities.[14]

Orthodox medicine—which can be defined as the type of medicine that is taught in medical schools, practiced in hospitals, and approved by the AMA, generates the greatest income because of its drugs, surgeons, and hospitals. Alternative medicine, as defined by the NIH, implies "any medical practice or intervention that does not have sufficient documentation in the United States to show that it is safe and effective against specific diseases and conditions; not generally taught in medical schools; and generally *not re-imbursable for third-party insurance billing*." So-called "alternative" treatments—such as nutritional, homeopathic, and herbal therapies; acupuncture, reflexology, and chiropractic—have been in use for centuries and are considered "mainstream" in Europe, India, China, and Japan.

When Dr. Robert Atkins switched from orthodox to alternative medicine, he decreased the number of pharmaceutical prescriptions in his practice by 90 percent. Experiences have led Dr. Atkins to conclude that medicine, as an organization, acts more out of economic than scientific motives; that medicine usually "denies truths learned only from empirical observation"; and that medicine does not necessarily accept the truth.

Doctors are not consciously withholding nutritional cures; they, too, are victims of the medical establishment. Medical schools receive grants from pharmaceutical companies, and courses in nutrition are not usually mandatory. Veterinarians must study nutrition to receive their license, yet medical students can go through their entire training without taking a single course. As a result, there is a natural tendency among physicians to reject nutrition deficiency as a direct cause of disease, to think of it as existing only in the extreme—as in scurvy, with nothing else in between. In 1984 the Committee on Nutrition in Medical Education reported that "Nutrition education programs in U.S. medical schools are largely inadequate to meet the present and future demands of the medical profession." If students were taught nutrition in medical school, there would be fewer diseases, less suffering, and much less money spent on health care.

---

[14] 1993 Statistics.

THE PHARMACEUTICAL COMPANIES

By their very nature, prescription drugs are the perfect product for a monopoly. Drugs are patented and available from only one manufacturer, and prices can be increased at the discretion of the company with few consumer complaints. How many people who are ill question the cost of drugs prescribed by their doctor? During the 1980s, inflation rose 58 percent and pharmaceutical companies managed to triple their prices. In 1990 the drug industry was the most profitable industry in America, with 13.6 percent annual profits, more than triple the average Fortune 500 company. The 1991 median profit of a Fortune pharmaceutical company was $592 million. Because the U.S. is the only major industrialized nation that does not regulate the prices or profits of drug companies, prescription drugs generally cost 25 to 40 percent more than in other countries. For three out of four elderly Americans, prescription drugs are their biggest expense.

Patents used to be in effect for seventeen years. Effective 8 June 1995, the FDA extended patent protection for a wide range of prescription drugs to *twenty years*, thus allowing brand-name drugs to keep their monopoly for *three extra years*. The FDA justified their actions by declaring they were simply implementing the 1994 General Agreement on Tariffs and Trade (GATT). Senator Pryor (of Arkansas) warned that the FDA's position would cost consumers billions of dollars:

"It means that there's going to be unjust enrichment for several drug companies. . . this was never intended by Congress. . . GATT's whole intention was to help consumers."

As of 8 June 1995 an estimated 109 drugs under existing patents will benefit from a longer protection period.

Pharmaceutical ad campaigns and the distribution of free samples usually determine the drugs doctors use to treat patients with. Advertisements in prominent medical journals are intentionally misleading, exaggerating a drug's benefits while downplaying its hazards in small print in the addendum. Although the FDA requires advertisers to present a "fair balance," Cheryl Graham, Acting Director of the FDA's Marketing Division, admits that one-half of the journal ads violate this standard. And since the FDA screens only 10 to 20 percent of all drug promotions, physicians are forced to take drug companies at their word.

The main sources of information for the FDA's regulation of drugs are the pharmaceutical companies. An inherent conflict of interest, the FDA simply evaluates the test results submitted by these companies. In addition, *a revolving door has been established between FDA executives and large companies in the food and drug business. In 1969 Congress revealed that thirty-seven of forty-nine top FDA officials left the agency to move into high corporate positions with the companies they had regulated. Another study disclosed that half of the high-ranking FDA officials had been employed as key executives in pharmaceutical companies immediately prior to joining the FDA. Half of these officials then went on to serve in an executive capacity for various pharmaceutical companies immediately after leaving the FDA. It is thus not surprising that in 1975, the General Accounting Office Study of FDA Officials reported that 150 FDA officials owned stocks in the companies they were supposed to be regulating, or that allegations of insider-trading of pharmaceutical stocks by FDA employees have been reported to the U.S. Securities and Exchange Commission.*

DRUGS VERSUS NUTRIENTS

Scientists and government regulators refuse to recognize the differences between drugs and nutrients:

Drugs are foreign to the body, and the body begins to detoxify and eliminate them immediately after they are ingested. Nutrients are essential to the body, which utilizes and stores them for future needs.

Drugs interfere with the metabolism or biochemical pathway of the body. Nutrients support the metabolism and biochemical pathways.

Drugs have immediate and specific therapeutic results. Nutrients have broader and much more gradual effects.

Drugs are often dangerous when taken in combination. Nutrients work best in combination.

Most drugs (with the exception of antibiotics) alleviate the symptoms, not the disease itself. Nutrients play essential roles in human health because they always deal with the underlying cause of the disease.

All drugs are toxicants, with many having serious side-
effects. Hundreds of people die every day from the inges-
tion of prescription drugs. Nutrients are natural to the body,
and it is their absence that leads to disease.

Since nutrient deficiencies are a component of most diseases,
when drugs are prescribed, the underlying cause of the disease is
masked and the disease usually worsens. At least 130,000 Americans are
killed annually from side effects of prescription drugs. In a counterclaim
filed in federal court against the FDA, Attorney Conrad LeBeau presented documented evidence of 1.3 million deaths in a ten-year period from
adverse drug reactions. So why is the FDA spending its time worrying
about health foods? How many people die from vitamins and herbs?
The only cases of people having serious side effects from vitamins are
those where the vitamins have been contaminated or used in megadoses
for months on end.

FATALITIES RESULTING FROM ALL MAJOR CATEGORIES OF PRESCRIPTION AND NON-PRESCRIPTION PHARMACEUTICAL DRUGS (not including illegal drugs) **IN THE U.S.** *

CATEGORIES	1983	1984	1985	1986	1987	1988	1989	1990
Analgesics	22	53	87	82	93	118	126	134
Anti-Depressants	19	57	90	100	105	135	140	159
Asthma Therapies	4	10	11	21	16	27	34	37
Cardiovascular (including blood pressure)	5	18	21	50	52	65	70	79
Sedatives/Hypnotics (sleeping pills/ tranquilizers)	11	51	62	61	48	77	78	72
Amphetamines	1	4	6	11	11	12	5	6
TOTAL	**62**	**193**	**227**	**325**	**325**	**434**	**453**	**487**

* Statistics do not reflect intentional suicides.

Data Taken From Annual Reports of
The American Association of Poison Control Centers

FATALITIES RESULTING FROM POISON BY VITAMINS IN THE U.S.

CATEGORIES	1983	1984	1985	1986	1987	1988	1989	1990
Multiple	0	0	0	0	0	0	0	0
Vitamin A	0	0	0	0	0	0	0	0
Niacin	0	0	0	0	0	0	0	I*
Pyridoxine	0	0	0	0	0	0	0	0
B-Complex	0	0	0	0	0	0	0	0
Vitamin C	0	0	0	0	0	0	0	0
Vitamin D	0	0	0	0	0	0	0	0
Vitamin E	0	0	0	0	0	0	0	0
Other	0	0	0	0	0	0	0	0
Unknown	0	0	0	0	0	0	0	0
TOTAL	**0**	**0**	**0**	**0**	**0**	**0**	**0**	**I**

*The death was probably more related to an underlying cardiovascular disease for which niacin was a treatment.

Data Taken From Annual Reports of
The American Association of Poison Control Centers

Certainly isolated cases of mild adverse reactions can be found to anything; the lack of reported adverse reactions to even megadoses of vitamins confirms they are not highly toxic. The purpose for having a government regulating agency is to keep dangerous products off the market. Instead the FDA approves lethal drugs while banning thousands of natural products and harassing the manufacturers and distributors of these products.

FDA INSISTS HALCION IS "SAFE AND EFFECTIVE"

The FDA has determined that Halcion is safe and effective, despite the fact that in 1990, the sleeping pill ranked first in the number of violent acts associated with 329 prescription drugs, and despite the fact that there have been consistent reports of amnesia, confusion, hostility, psychosis, depression, dependence, and even death since it was first marketed in the United States in 1983.

Halcion was withdrawn from the Dutch market in 1978, and from France and Italy in 1987. Britain determined that the psychiatric risks were too great and banned its use in 1991; eight other countries followed suit. Yet both Upjohn (its manufacturer) and the FDA have dismissed concerns over safety. In 1991 Upjohn made $104 million on Halcion sales in the U.S. and $133 million abroad—it's their second biggest money-maker.

In a recent FDA report (obtained by the Freedom of Information Act), FDA investigators concluded that Upjohn had "engaged in an ongoing pattern of misconduct with Halcion": Upjohn misled the FDA about the significance of patients' adverse reactions, misreported side-effects data to French and Japanese regulators, and established an "ongoing campaign to discredit or neutralize any individual or publication reporting adverse information about Halcion." Although Upjohn knew in 1982 that "long-term use [of Halcion] was both dangerous and medically untenable," company officials "misrepresented the data" to prevent the FDA from limiting prescriptions to fourteen days. In the Physicians' Desk Reference (PDR), which lists information about prescription drugs provided by the manufacturer, Upjohn instructed doctors to prescribe Halcion for up to thirty days—Upjohn did not admit until 1992 that there could be serious side effects if Halcion was used for more than one week to ten days. According to the FDA report, Upjohn "chose to disregard the potential harm of inappropriate use, in order to gain additional sales (profits)." *Despite this damaging report, the FDA continues to allow Halcion to be marketed in the United States.*

FOOD ADDITIVES

The FDA regularly approves potentially cancer-causing food preservatives and drugs, which has corresponded with the spiraling cancer rate over the last fifty years. Thousands of chemical additives used for the purpose of coloring, preserving, and flavoring our foods *have not* been tested by the FDA. Currently it is believed that one in three Americans will experience cancer at some point during their lifetime.

There is growing evidence in chronic conditions such as asthma, allergy, mood disturbances, migraine, and hyperactivity, that additives are undermining our health. Although additives have tripled in less than a generation, crucial issues such as overall additive exposure, interacting exposures, and effects over a lifetime have not been addressed. The FDA regulates specific additives only when powerful evidence against one arises, and then usually at the insistence of outside scientists or consumer groups. A clear example of FDA negligence was its refusal to ban sulfites, despite the knowledge that sulfites provoked attacks in 5 to 10 percent of asthma patients and in an unknown number of other people. The FDA did not ban sulfites until July of 1986, after fifteen sulfite fatalities had been documented. And what about nitrates? Recent studies demonstrate that hot dogs, which are high in sodium and nitrates, pose a serious risk to children: According to one study at the University of Southern California School of Medicine, children who consume twelve or more hot dogs a month have nine times the risk of contracting childhood leukemia. How many children will die from cancer before the FDA regulates the usage of nitrates?

BIO-ENGINEERED FOOD

As current regulations stand, biotechnology firms can sell genetically-altered food with practically zero interference from the government. The FDA has not labeled or imposed specific regulations on bio-engineered food, once again protecting industry instead of the consumer. The food industry fears labeling a product as genetically-altered will scare away consumers. Americans could be eating a potato with a chicken gene in it and be totally unaware.

In April of 1994, the FDA's food-advisory committee approved the first genetically-engineered tomato, the MacGregor Flavr Savr, for consumer consumption. The "Flavr Savr" is supposed to last longer than natural tomatoes. Although the FDA advisory-committee determined this new tomato to be safe, several of the participants expressed concern about biotech regulations for future genetically-engineered foods: The

FDA does not plan to require companies to notify them when a new, genetically-engineered product is going to be marketed; companies will be required to apprise the FDA *only* if a new food differs substantially from the original or poses any health risk.

Many of the biotech crops are being genetically-engineered for herbicide tolerance. Calgene is testing the chemical weedkiller bromoxynil on cottonseed. According to the Environmental Protection Agency, bromoxynil causes birth defects in laboratory animals and may subject farm workers to a similar risk. FDA Commissioner David Kessler claims: "We're going to assure the safety of all foods, whether produced by traditional breeding or genetic engineering." How can the FDA possibly ensure the safety of *unlabeled* bio-engineered foods that look the same as ordinary fruits and vegetables?

Is it a coincidence that the largest pesticide companies in the world are also pharmaceutical companies? Drug pesticide companies such as Dow, Ciba-Geigy, Monsanto, Hoechst, Bayer, Dupont, ICI and Rhone-Poulenc first decided to insert genes into food crops, in order for these crops to be able to tolerate more pesticides and herbicides. Our soil and food supply are being saturated with poisons for the increased profits of the drug/pesticide companies.

Genetically-engineered milk has been marketed *without labels* in grocery stores throughout the U.S. since February of 1994. Monsanto Corporation has taken a cow hormone and recombined its genetic structure to create a new hormone—bovine growth hormone (rBGH)—which artificially stimulates cows to increase milk production by 20 percent. Although the FDA insists "the milk [containing rBGH] is identical in every way to non-supplemented," rBGH has been shown to increase mastitis infections in cows, which, in turn, requires increased doses of antibiotics. Dr. Samuel Epstein has accused the FDA of ignoring published research that links hormone-injected cows with increased risk of breast cancer. *Is it a coincidence that Deputy Commissioner Michael Taylor, a former counsel for Monsanto, wrote the FDA guidelines that ruled out mandatory labeling for the growth hormone?* Consumers have been so upset over the unlabeled bio-engineered milk that the governors in Vermont and Maine signed bills that will require mandatory labeling for milk products with rBGH hormones. Other states have yet to follow suit.

On 14 December 1994 the European Council of Ministers imposed a ban through the year 2000 on the commercial use of rBGH.

Once again, we have a clear example of the FDA's double standard—authorizing unlabeled, potentially cancer causing bio-engineered food and milk, while banning dietary supplements because of "unsubstantiated labeling."

CHAPTER EIGHT

AN UNDERCOVER DICTATORSHIP

Unless we put medical freedom into the Constitution, the time will come when medicine will organize into an undercover dictatorship.

Dr. Benjamin Rush
Surgeon General of George
Washington's armies

Certainly there is the need for an agency to regulate prescription drugs; however, vitamin and nutritional supplements fall into an entirely different category and should never have been put under the authority of the FDA. The FDA continues to deny the existence of thousands of articles published in the scientific literature that support the use of therapeutic applications of nutritional supplements.[15] As a regulatory agency, the FDA operating style is adversarial—ensuring

---

[15] Brian Leibovitz, Ph.D, Editor-in-Chief of the *Journal of Optimal Nutrition*, wrote to FDA Commissioner David Kessler, Deputy Commissioner Gary Dykstra, and the Head of Nutrition at the FDA, Dr. Vanderveen, offering to send complimentary articles of the latest nutrition-related literature. Despite Leibovitz's two letters and dozens of follow-up phone calls, he did not receive a response from any of these officials.

nutritionally sound dietary practices, which varies from individual to individual, cannot be regulated by police-like actions.

KESSLER'S REIGN OF TERROR

David Kessler became FDA Commissioner shortly after the 1989 generic drug scandal, which involved the conviction of four FDA employees for taking illegal bribes from pharmaceutical companies. In a 1994 "60 Minutes" interview, Kessler explained, "We had to win back the trust of the American people."

Kessler seems to have planned his political career early on. He studied for a medical and law degree simultaneously, followed by a pediatrics residency at night while working on food and drug legislation in Senator Orrin Hatch's Capitol Hill office during the day. He frequently appears on CNN's "Larry King Live" and network news broadcasts, where he portrays the FDA as protecting consumers from big business.

Yet Kessler's continuous campaign to increase FDA regulatory powers and his denigration of nutritional supplements—"We are slipping back to the turn of the century, when snake oil salesmen roamed about"—demonstrate his indifference to constitutional rights and freedom of choice in health care. *The reality is that Commissioner Kessler has sanctioned the execution of totalitarian political tactics, violations of First Amendment free speech rights, and the dissemination of inaccurate nutritional information.*

FDA CONFISCATES BLACK CURRENT OIL FROM TRACO LABS

The FDA attempted to circumvent the Proxmire Amendment by turning from drug potency arguments to enforcement attempts. The agency contended that any dietary supplement *added* to a capsule or tablet was a "food additive" (as in the case of evening primrose oil). Under this theory, the FDA could present an affidavit from one of its scientists stating that experts generally did not regard the product as safe. *The actual safety of the product was never at issue.*

On 27 January 1993 Traco Labs, Inc. won a federal court decision on their "encapsuled product"—black current oil. Back in 1988, the FDA had instructed a U.S. marshal to confiscate two drums of black current oil as they were en route for Traco Labs in Champaign, Illinois. The FDA had determined the product an "unsafe food additive." Like evening primrose oil and other softgel oils, black current oil was in danger of being classified as a food additive and permanently removed from the market. At the first federal hearing, in April of 1991, Judge Baker sided with Traco:

> "... The FDA has failed to explain how placing black cur-
> rent oil in a gelatin container converts the black current oil
> into a food additive. In this case there is no proof that the
> black current oil affects the characteristics of another food or
> becomes a component of another food. Allowing the FDA to
> call a single ingredient placed into a gelatin capsule a "food
> additive" would eliminate any distinction between "food"
> and "food additive"... This court cannot permit the agency
> charged with enforcing the Act to redefine its terms."

It took Traco four and one-half years and untold sums of money to beat the FDA, demonstrating why most small manufacturers cannot defend their product. In June of 1992, the FDA challenged another manufacturer of black current oil, Oakmont/Health in Massachusetts, with selling a food additive. Once again, the federal court asserted that the oil could not be designated as a food additive just because it was encapsulated. Despite these setbacks, the FDA asked the Department of Justice to overturn both cases in the Supreme Court; the Solicitor General refused to file the FDA's petitions.

Obviously, the FDA does not expect to be crossed in court. In *Food & Drug Insider Report*, an FDA enforcement staffer was quoted as saying: "We have depended on the ability to selectively target companies ... and to issue findings without fear of being second-guessed by some tinhorn judge."

CONSUMERS OUTRAGED BY SEIZURE OF CoQ10 FROM AUSTIN WHOLE FOODS MARKET

Coenzyme Q10 (CoQ10) has also been a recent target. An oil-soluble vitamin, CoQ10 helps the body's cells convert food and oxygen into ATP (adenosine triphosphate), a chemical that all tissues require to function properly. CoQ10 is especially beneficial for heart problems, as supplements have been shown to significantly increase the recovery time of a person suffering from heart disease. The treatment of choice in Japan, CoQ10 is a widely prescribed heart medication in Sweden, Italy, Denmark, and Canada. More than one thousand research papers have been published on it worldwide, and six international symposia have documented its safety, efficacy, and lack of side effects. Karl Folkers, who has researched CoQ10 since 1957, was issued an IND number in 1970 and has submitted numerous studies to the FDA demonstrating its safety and efficacy. Yet the FDA still insists that CoQ10 is an unsafe food additive.

On 11 February 1992 the Texas Department of Health confiscated CoQ10 from an Austin Whole Foods Market. Austin residents, who were committed to holistic health care, phoned and wrote letters of complaint to their congressmen, the Texas Department of Health, and the FDA. Former Texan Ed Fitzjarrell, president of Metabolic Maintenance Products (based in California), flew to Austin and met with the Texas Department of Health. He agreed to file a GRAS petition for CoQ10 (which costs anywhere from $50,000 to $100,000). Although Fitzjarrell's company produced just 2 percent of all the CoQ10 sold in the U.S., he opposed the FDA's ban for the following reason:

"I'm just a tiny encapsulator. None of my product was seized. Why am I coming forward? I'm here because of the big picture. The big picture. If CoQ10 fails in Texas, within a year it will be banned from all other states. On a personal level, I know people who use it and need it."

"B-VITAMIN BUST" - THE FDA RAIDS DR. JONATHAN WRIGHT'S ALTERNATIVE MEDICINE CLINIC

The armed raid of Dr. Jonathan Wright's Kent, Washington office in May of 1992 is another example of how the FDA has tried to "protect" the public against "unsafe" products when there is *no evidence* that the product is unsafe.

Considered one of the world's experts in nutritional biochemistry, Dr. Wright received his undergraduate degree at Harvard and his medical degree from the University of Michigan. Dr. Wright specializes in nutritional medicine, using vitamins, minerals, and amino acids to successfully treat a variety of ailments. In August of 1991, Dr. Wright filed a lawsuit against the FDA for seizure of a dispensary stock of L-tryptophan. Within three weeks, the FDA began investigating his clinic: FDA employees checked the dumpster periodically for evidence of vitamin products with foreign labels, and visited the clinic posing as patients.

Nothing could have prepared Dr. Wright for the morning of 6 May 1992 when twelve FDA agents in flak vests and ten King County policemen knocked down the doors of his Tahoma Clinic in an armed "commando-style" raid. Bursting into the clinic from three directions, police officers and FDA agents pointed guns at the staff, ordering, "Get your hands up!" Receptionist Marge Murphy recalls: "They broke through the main door yelling, and one of them pointed a gun in my face." When another employee, Patty Hoops, attempted to call her attorney, a police officer ripped the telephone off the wall and threw Patty into a chair, injuring her elbow.

Dr. Wright arrived at the clinic a few minutes past 9:00 AM, after the officers and agents had forced their way in. The FDA presented a search warrant, allowed him to make one phone call to his attorney, and then began their fourteen-hour search and seizure. The search warrant authorized agents to seize all drugs labeled in a foreign language, to confiscate all literature describing or promoting the subject compounds, to seize all documents, including patient records, that related to dispensing the vitamin products, as well as confiscation of "all additional records, whether they be in the form of documentary records, magnetic disks, hard disks, or maintained in any other form."

The police officers (which included three sergeants and one supervisor), had not even looked at the contents of the search warrant; they were pushovers for the FDA, cooperating fully in this SWAT-team style search and seizure. And for what reason? To seize dietary supplements.

FDA agents seized a Vitamin B_{12} complex manufactured in Germany, which Dr. Wright used to treat patients with allergies—the German form of Vitamin B_{12} is the only injectable vitamin that does not contain preservatives or additives.[16]

Agents seized $100,000 worth in medicines, office supplies, and equipment: patient and employee records; banking statements; payroll records; injectable, preservative-free vitamins, mineral and glandular extracts; noninvasive allergy and sensitivity-testing equipment; instruction and training manuals; postage stamps, address books, correspondence, diaries, rolodexes, telephone toll records and messages; and the entire printed contents of the hard drive on the clinic's central computer system.

Refusing to take responsibility for what soon became known as the "B-Vitamin Bust," the FDA asked a federal judge to seal portions of the affidavit that explained the reasons for the FDA's action. Patients of Dr. Wright and the local news media were furious. Several Seattle television stations aired a videotape taken by a patient, which depicted FDA agents, dressed in bulletproof vests, bursting into the clinic and com-

---

[16] Vitamin B_{12} is not a drug; the German form of this complex is used throughout the U.S.

manding employees to freeze; local news stations showed angry patients picketing in front of Wright's office. Editorials appeared in newspapers throughout the state: "If there is any plausible excuse for the Gestapo-like tactics used in a raid on a Kent alternative medicine clinic, it had better be forthcoming and fast," the *Seattle Post-Intelligencer* declared. Within twenty-four hours of the raid, 2,000 letters were faxed to President Bush from irate citizens and people as far away as London and Brazil. Citizens For Health, a national lobbying group on issues of alternative and mainstream medicine, received numerous telephone calls and letters from worried Americans throughout the country. The required number of faxes to warrant the attention of the President is 20,000; Citizens For Health organized a fax-sending mission to the White House to make sure the White House received at least 20,000 faxes on the raid. Dr. Wright participated in a Seattle television talk show for nine hours and the switchboards lit up. Public interest in the case finally forced the judge to unseal the FDA affidavit—it had been sealed for ten days.

A few weeks after the raid, Dr. Wright—wearing an "I survived an FDA raid" t-shirt—recalled his experience at an American College for the Advancement of Medicine (ACAM) meeting. He spoke of how the FDA was now denying they had been armed, despite the fact that there were twenty-four eyewitnesses and a videotape containing at-the-scene footage; of how his only motivation was to improve health care with vitamins and alternative therapies; of how he lost ten pounds in ten days after the raid.

The United States federal government is drawing guns on its citizens for taking vitamins. What was the motivation behind the FDA's raid? The agency claimed "drugs were being manufactured" at Wright's office. Vitamin-B drugs? Is this how the FDA protects the public? On a call-in television show a few days after the raid, FDA Commissioner David Kessler described the FDA's actions as "standard operating procedure"; the officers "had to protect themselves." How can the FDA justify such extreme behavior? Since the raid, Dr. Wright and his wife have, upon returning from abroad, been singled out in customs lines: Not only has their luggage been searched but they themselves have been taken to a room and strip-searched. Our freedoms are threatened as they have never been.

FDA BANS L-TRYPTOPHAN

L-tryptophan is an amino acid supplement widely used as a stress reducer and treatment for insomnia. The L-tryptophan ban is yet another illustration of how the FDA and pharmaceutical companies conspire to keep beneficial natural ingredients off the market.

In late 1989, the FDA recalled all L-tryptophan products following the deaths of thirty-eight people from EMS (Eosinophilia Myalgia Syndrome), which the FDA associated with their intake of L-tryptophan. After a thorough investigation, the CDC reported in the *New England Journal of Medicine* in 1990 that the deaths were not caused by L-tryptophan but by a contaminant contained in a few batches produced by a Japanese company (Showa Denko).

The official FDA publication, *FDA Consumer*, also reported the CDC's findings on the contaminated L-tryptophan shipment:

"Epidemiologic studies indicated that a vast majority of the EMS cases were linked to products containing L-tryptophan produced by Showa Denko K.K. However, **it appears that the problem is not with the amino acid itself, but rather with the product becoming contaminated as a result of a change in the firm's manufacturing process.**"

The FDA may actually be at fault for not inspecting the Showa Denko shipment of L-tryptophan: The German equivalent of the FDA identified the contamination and banned the shipment from Germany.

To date the FDA has refused to re-introduce L-tryptophan to the U.S. marketplace, although its double standard is obvious as L-tryptophan is allowed to be added to baby foods, hospital tube feedings, and pet products. Commissioner Kessler attempted to justify the FDA's ban when he told Congress in July of 1993: "The exact cause of EMS and an understanding of how it develops have not been established." Apparently Dr. Kessler had not read the CDC's article in the *New England Journal of Medicine* or his own agency's *FDA Consumer*.

L-tryptophan produces serotonin, an important brain neurotransmitter. Since the 1960s, L-tryptophan had been sold in tablet, capsule and powdered forms as a nutritional supplement. Some of its noted benefits are: reduction in pain sensitivity; relief in many cases of depression, anxiety and stress; and facilitation of natural sleep. In a twenty-year period, fourteen million people took L-tryptophan regularly with no reports of toxicity.

During the 1980s, L-tryptophan sales in the U.S. steadily increased, up to $180 million per year. The pharmaceutical companies did not benefit from these revenues. Since its 1989 recall, those who had depended on L-tryptophan have been forced to choose either addictive, dangerous, and expensive drugs such as Xanax, Valium, Halcion, Dalmane, Codeine, Prozac, and Anafranil—or live with their pain.

The FDA continues to issue deceptive statements, raising "serious questions" about the nutritional value and safety of amino acids. Gary Dykstra, Deputy Commissioner for Regulatory Affairs of the FDA, announced in July 1992 that his committee would recommend that the FDA regulate amino acids as prescription drugs. What pharmaceutical company is going to invest at least $230 million (the cost of the drug approval process) in a "drug" that cannot be patented? If the FDA had its way, it is conceivable that amino acids would be taken off the market permanently.

Garry F. Gordon, M.D., co-founder of the American College of Advancement in Medicine, noted that the FDA's campaign against L-tryptophan dates back over a decade, when the FDA lost a courtroom battle to remove L-tryptophan from the shelves:

"As we left the courtroom, they [FDA] said, 'Well, you beat us this time, but we have lots of other avenues and we will get it stopped.'"

When contaminated foods and over-the-counter drugs are discovered, once they are identified and corrected, the FDA allows them back into the marketplace. Clearly the L-tryptophan-EMS affair should have been treated as a contaminated food. Instead dangerous prescription drugs are increasing in use because the public is being denied access to a safe and effective amino acid.

NUTRITION LABELING AND EDUCATION ACT (NLEA)

In 1990 Congress approved NLEA, which authorized the FDA to standardize and improve nutritional claims on outdated food labels, in order to give meaning to terms such as "lowfat" and "low sodium." Congress did not intend for the FDA to use NLEA to restrict the availability of dietary supplements. In fact, Congress included an amendment to NLEA that instructed the FDA to set up separate labeling guidelines for dietary supplements. The statute specifically stated that the FDA could recommend a different standard and approval procedure for supplements. In its restrictive interpretation of NLEA, the FDA has used arbitrary powers Congress never intended for it to have, enforcing laws that have not been legislated.

When the FDA began implementing NLEA in December of 1991, they only approved one nutritional claim—calcium to prevent osteoporosis in White and Asian Women. To date, only one other claim—folic acid for the prevention of birth defects—has been approved (and only after enormous public pressure on the FDA). Both the Public Health Service and CDC had recommended folic acid for women of child-bearing age two years prior to the FDA's October 1993 approval of the health claim.

FDA ASKS CONGRESS FOR POLICE-STATE POWERS

In 1992 the FDA attempted to have Congress pass legislation that would have allowed them to conduct armed raids similar to what occurred in Dr. Wright's clinic, legislation that would have given them legitimate police-state powers. The FDA proposed that it use the "significant scientific agreement" standard: The level of proof required for dietary health claims was so unrealistic in the degree of scientific consensus and clinical data required, that almost all existing claims would have been eliminated.

The FDA asked Congress to impose personal fines of up to $250,000 and business fines of up to $1 million for violations of *their interpretation* of NLEA. They also requested authorization for "seizure and detention of any food, drug, device or cosmetic that is in violation of the FDA." Current law authorizes seizure of any food, drug or cosmetic for *specified reasons* and detention of any device for *specified reasons*. This legislation would have given the FTC the authority to restrict advertising and marketing of nutritional products that did not conform with NLEA regulations by imposing severe penalties on liable parties. The Senate version of the proposed Congressional bill would have imposed fines up to $2 million.[17]

Had the above proposals passed, the FDA would have been empowered with *police-state powers* to search and seize products without probable cause or due process; to hand out heavy civil penalties; to legally enter a company's facilities and subpoena all its records, including trade secrets; and to embargo any product for thirty days without giving the business an opportunity for a hearing. State agencies would have also had increased enforcement power to implement severe civil penalties.

---

[17] The proposed Congressional bill was entitled H.R. 3642; the Senate version, S.2135.

The FDA proposals would have severely restricted amino acids, medicinal herbs, and other unapproved nutrients, making them available only by prescription. Companies would have been prohibited from making health claims on their product labels without scientific research: Claiming that fiber can help prevent cancer would have been illegal; a brand name such as "Health Valley" would have been in jeopardy. To further restrict nutritional information, the FDA warned it would prohibit "third-party" organizations from making health claims associated with nutritional products. Small firms, those who sell their products through natural food stores, would not have survived.

Some of the dietary supplements that would have been restricted or banned by the FDA are: essential fatty acids— evening primrose oil, borage oil, black current seed oil, flax seed oil; herbs—such as echinacea, ginkgo, garlic, pau d'arco, valerian, ginseng and other popular chinese herbs; all amino acids—such as L-lysine, L-glutamine; enzymes—such as bromelain and quercitin; co-enzyme Q10; diet formulas; antioxidant formulas; and PABA. The potency of vitamins would have been dramatically reduced to those levels found in food. High potency vitamins, such as Vitamin C in doses of 1000 milligrams or more, would have been regulated as drugs, requiring a doctor's prescription.

The FDA even petitioned to replace the Recommended Daily Allowance (RDA) on labels to Reference Daily Intake (RDI); RDI requirements are less than the RDA. U.S. RDAs are extremely misleading because they are based on the concept of single-nutrient diseases, such as scurvy and rickets—RDAs are not based on the amount of nutrients needed to maintain optimum health. Since the medical establishment has always maintained that to exceed the RDAs is potentially dangerous, many consumers mistakenly assume that the RDA for a nutrient is sufficient for good health. Had the FDA been successful in switching the standard for nutrient intake from RDA to RDI, nutritional deficiencies in the United States would have increased.

At a 1992 FDA Task Force meeting, its leader, Gary Dykstra, told the health food industry they could expect heavy enforcement activities in the near future.

ANGRY CITIZENS DEMAND THAT CONGRESS RESTRICT FDA ENFORCEMENT POWERS

Consumers were so outraged by the FDA's proposed legislation that they wrote more letters to Congress on this issue than on any other. Both the *Los Angeles Times* and the *New York Times* reported that the number one issue in Washington in 1992 through 1994, as measured by congressional mail, was dietary supplements. Groups that asked Congress to redirect the FDA included Citizens For Health, Council For Responsible Nutrition, the Nutritional Health Alliance, the American Herbal Products Association, and the National Nutritional Foods Association.

Influenced more by political action committees (PACS) than by angry constituents, Congressmen Henry Waxman and John Dingell introduced the FDA's proposed legislation in Congress. In May of 1992, Senator Edward Kennedy promoted the same proposals in a Senate hearing. A few weeks later, Senator Orrin Hatch countered with a new bill, The Health Freedom Act, which was designed to prevent the FDA from classifying dietary supplements as drugs or food additives solely because they exceeded the level of potency desired by the FDA.

Senator Hatch:

"There is a growing body of research that indicates that dietary supplements can help promote health and prevent certain diseases. In our free market system, consumers should be able to purchase dietary supplements and companies should be free to sell these products so long as the labeling and advertising is truthful and non-misleading and there exists a reasonable scientific basis for product claims."

Shortly after the introduction of the Hatch legislation, FDA and state officials in Senator Hatch's home state of Utah conducted a raid on a dietary supplement firm, Nature's Way Products, and seized their supply of evening primrose oil.

Working with the various consumer health groups, Senator Hatch managed to persuade Congress in the fall of 1992 to extend the deadline for regulation of dietary supplements for one year. A few months later Senator Hatch and Congressman Bill Richardson sponsored the Dietary Supplement Health and Education Act, to establish a regulatory framework for vitamins, minerals, herbs, amino acids, and other dietary supplements; to protect supplements from being arbitrarily removed from the market as food additives; and to protect consumers by guaranteeing their right to obtain safe nutritional products and truthful, science-based information about their benefits.

In his introductory statement for the House bill, Rep. Bill Richardson stated:

"The exploding costs and inadequacies of our current health system have caused many citizens and health professionals to explore and investigate the use and efficacy of complementary and alternative forms of health care. The great interest in dietary supplements reflects the desire of our citizens to have more control over their own health care decisions. We must consider, as many of our constituents have, the potential value of dietary supplementation in order to prevent disease and to maintain health and wellness. Scientific research findings continue to show that supplementation of certain nutrients can significantly reduce the incidence of chronic diseases."

Siding with the FDA and the orthodox medical establishment, the *New York Times* dubbed the Hatch-Richardson legislation "The 1993 Snake Oil Protection Act." This "establishment" newspaper asserted that the dietary supplement industry was using scare tactics and misinformation to "rally thousands of health-minded Americans to support legislation that would actually deprive consumers of reliable health information"—when, in fact, it was the FDA and mainstream media who were responsible for deliberate deceptions and inaccuracies.

On 10 May 1994 Commissioner Kessler adamantly argued before a Senate committee that the manufacturers of dietary supplements meet the "significant scientific agreement" standard before making health claims about their products. He claimed that the FDA had "very little data" on the effectiveness of vitamins, and must therefore "insist on rigorous testing." This from a man who had professed in 1993 that "The public can be assured that access [to dietary supplements] will not be altered" by the FDA.

THE DIETARY SUPPLEMENT HEALTH AND EDUCATION ACT OF 1994

It was not until October of 1994 that both the Senate and Congress approved a compromise bill, the Dietary Supplement Health and Education Act of 1994, which guaranteed consumers' access to dietary supplements but also preserved the FDA's right to regulate claims used to sell them. This legislation prohibits manufacturers from making health claims for their products for four years while a

Commission on Dietary Supplements studies the issue. After two years, the commission is expected to make recommendations, which the Secretary of Health & Human Services and Congress will review. Until these recommendations are made, manufacturers have to provide the FDA with safety evidence seventy-five days before a product is introduced into the market; if the FDA does not specifically disapprove the supplement within the seventy-five-day period, the product can be marketed, although the FDA still has the option to remove the product. Under the Dietary Supplement Health and Education Act, manufacturers are allowed to distribute reprints of preliminary scientific studies that describe potential health benefits of supplements, and can make nutritional claims such as "Vitamin A is necessary for good vision."

Less than two months after the enactment of the Dietary Supplement Health and Education Act, the FDA violated the new law by conducting raids against clinics, labs, and distributors of nutritional supplements *without giving the companies the ten day notice required by Congress*. In early February 1995, FDA agents raided Independent Testing Labs, Inc., an analytical laboratory in Grand Island, Nebraska. Agents seized $55,000 in vitamins manufactured by Standard Process, a midwest supplement manufacturer that had been in business for more than four decades and had never received a citation or warning letter from the FDA. That same month, FDA agents raided Bio-Mechanics Clinic and Health Store in Aberdeen, Idaho, seizing the clinic's herbal supplements, testing equipment, patient files, and ledgers.

The FDA continues to remove alternative health books from the marketplace. By their very nature, dietary supplements must be marketed so that the consumer is informed of their health and disease-prevention benefits. Yet according to the FDA's interpretation of NLEA, designated dietary literature is an extension of product labeling; the FDA insists that displaying books with products constitutes "technically labeling" as the products can then be branded as drugs.

The FDA has prevented Nutricology from selling the book *Miracle Cure: Organic Germanium* by Kasuhiko Asai, since Nutricology markets germanium supplements. In August of 1994, New York's Ellis Island Immigrant Museum closed part of a book exhibit on immigrant health traditions after receiving criticism about its alternative health care display. Victor Herbert, M.D., orthodox medicine's favorite spokesman, wrote a letter to the superintendent of the Statue of Liberty National Monument and Ellis Island, complaining that alternative health care books promoted health fraud.[18] He asserted that the reference book,

---

[18] Victor Herbert, M.D. is the author of *The Vitamin Pushers: How the Health Food Industry is Selling America a Bill of Goods*.

Alternative Medicine: The Definitive Guide—which had been part of the museum's display—"was organized quackery." *Alternative Medicine* utilized the expertise of 380 medical doctors.

In a revealing September 1994 article in *Publishers Weekly*, publishers admitted to passing up alternative medicine books due to their fear of the FDA. One publisher, who insisted on anonymity, told *Publishers Weekly*: "It's getting to the point of censorship. The threat of FDA action is affecting what publishers are willing to put their name on and what booksellers are willing to stock." Publishing professionals would not comment "on the record" about the FDA.

For over thirty years, the FDA has campaigned to expand its regulatory powers over nutritional supplements, disregarding Congressional mandates to limit its authority. Given the FDA's history, there is no reason to believe that the passage of the <u>Dietary Supplement Health and Education Act of 1994</u> will prevent the FDA from future attempts to regulate vitamins and nutrients as prescription drugs.

CHAPTER NINE

ACQUIRED IMMUNE DEFICIENCY SYNDROME

The most important and urgent task for politicians, both in Government and Parliament, is to force scientists to speak clearly, precisely and honestly about the AIDS epidemic. Half-truths, wishful thinking, flawed scientific hypotheses and deceptions have been perpetrated by scientists, and allowed to flourish as conventional wisdom, aided and abetted by editors of scientific and medical journals. The deceptions must be exposed with maximum publicity . . . The longer the truth is obscured from the public, and the greater the multitude of innocent people who die most horribly as a result, the more ferocious will be the explosion of hatred and revenge against those guilty of perpetuating the deceptions.

Problems Associated With Aids
British House of Commons Report
Session 1986-87

SMALLPOX VACCINE DISTRIBUTED IN COUNTRIES WHERE AIDS IS NOW RAMPANT

"Smallpox Vaccine 'Triggered AIDS Virus'" was the shocking front-page headline of the 11 May 1987 issue of the *London Times*. In 1972, the World Health Organization (WHO) had conducted large scale smallpox vaccinations in central Africa, Uganda, Haiti, Brazil, and Japan, the same areas where AIDS was now rampant. In the United States, where recruits to the American armed services are immunized for smallpox as a precaution against biological warfare, a nineteen-year-old developed AIDS just twenty and a half weeks after a routine vaccination. It had long been speculated but never printed in England's establishment press that the WHO's smallpox vaccination program was the real origin of the AIDS epidemic.

For over a year, experts at the WHO had been discussing privately the link between their anti-smallpox campaign and the occurrence of AIDS. If the use of the live smallpox vaccine had activated a dormant HIV virus, it would account for the heterosexual spread of AIDS in Central Africa, the relative absence of infection among children who did not receive the vaccination, as well as explain why Brazil had the highest incidence of AIDS in South America. Afterall, contaminated polio vaccines in the early 1960s resulted in brain cancer SV-40 virus; contaminated swine flu vaccines in the 1970s caused polio-like diseases. Could it be possible that AIDS was man–made?

In 1972, the same year the WHO's smallpox vaccination program began, the WHO had advertised in their monthly newsletter, the *Bulletin*, for volunteers (scientists) to create and study AIDS-like viruses:

"An attempt should be made to see if viruses can in fact exert selective effects on immune function. The possibility should be looked into that the immune response to the virus itself may be impaired if the infecting virus damages, more or less selectively, the cell responding to the virus."

In its 1987 report, *Problems Associated With AIDS*, the British House of Commons speculated that AIDS was man-made:

"Every biological scientist who has dispassionately studied the virus and the epidemic knows that the origins of the virus could lie in the developments of modern biology, just as the origins of the nuclear bomb was modern physics."

U.S. newspapers did not print the explosive *London Times* story, though the Associated Press was most certainly aware of it. Likewise, the American mainstream media has not, for the most part, reported the research and theories of those who believe that AIDS is man-made, or that AIDS is not caused by the HIV virus.

Robert B. Strecker, M.D., Ph.D., who has researched the origins of AIDS extensively, theorizes (with documentation) that scientists with the National Cancer Institute (NCI) and WHO created the AIDS virus in NCI laboratories in Fort Detrick, Maryland. He speculates that the AIDS virus is a combination of two bovine or sheep viruses cultured in human cells in a laboratory. There will never be a vaccine, according to Strecker, since the numerous AIDS viruses have the ability to recombine with the genes of any cell they enter more times than we can count: There are over 9,000 possible AIDS viruses, and trillions of possible genetic combinations. The common cold, for which there is no cure, recombines less frequently. The NIH calls Strecker's theory "bad science."

If Dr. Strecker's hypothesis is so ridiculous, then why has he been censored by prestigious American and European medical journals, by network television and radio, and by major newspapers? When he attempted to advertise his AIDS video, *The Strecker Memorandum*, why was Dr. Strecker denied television and radio advertising time? If he is talking nonsense, why the need for censorship? Give the public some credit and let the American people discern what's real and what isn't.

Since the early 1990s, the *London Times* has been openly critical of the American medical establishment's theory that the HIV virus causes AIDS; in fact, the *Times* concurs with California biologist Peter Duesberg, an international expert in retroviruses, who believes that AIDS is neither caused by HIV nor as widespread as the NIH and WHO estimate. For over a decade, the U.S. government has been telling us that the African green monkey transferred AIDS to man through natural means. Africans have been eating the green monkey for thousands of years; why did it take so long for AIDS to develop? Dr. Duesberg insists the green monkey theory is ludicrous. And there are many respected scientists who agree with Duesberg.

BRITISH HOUSE OF COMMONS REPORT ON AIDS

The Social Services Committee, authors of the British House of Common's report on AIDS, urged politicians back in 1987 to speak honestly about the AIDS epidemic:

"The scale of deceptions and misinformation perpetrated by virologists, clinicians and editors of scientific and medical journals about the infectivity of genital secretions is astonishing; having assumed for a variety of motives that AIDS is a sexually transmitted disease, like syphilis or gonorrhea, a negligible research effort has gone into the critical matter of transmission."

The House of Commons report accused medical and scientific editors of misleading their professional colleagues about the nature and severity of the AIDS epidemic: "By selecting authors to write 'safe' editorials and review articles, they have perpetuated dangerous misconceptions." *The absence of investigative reporting into the scientific scandals surrounding AIDS indicated that journalists were afraid to question the conventional wisdom.*
        The British House of Commons published this report eight years ago, yet similar questions are apparently still too controversial for the U.S. government to acknowledge. How can we know what to believe and what not to believe when information is being censored? It has been hypothesized that American homosexuals were given AIDS through hepatitis-B vaccines introduced in 1978—AIDS didn't exist in the U.S. prior to that year. In 1981, 4 percent of those receiving the hepatitis vaccine were AIDS-infected, and by 1984 the percentage had increased to 60 percent. The CDC has refused to give out figures after 1984, and the U.S. Department of Justice has since buried hepatitis vaccine studies.
        In the Surgeon General's "Understanding AIDS" pamphlet (issued in 1988), we are told the main ways the disease can be transmitted are through oral, anal or vaginal sex, the sharing of drug needles, and to babies of infected mothers before or during birth. "Any exchange of infected blood, semen or vaginal fluids can spread the virus and place you at risk." We are told we won't get AIDS from saliva, sweat, tears or urine, and that we won't get AIDS from a kiss. How can we be sure the Surgeon General's report is accurate?

GLOBAL FORECASTS

During the summer of 1994, the WHO reported that 16 million adults and 1 million children had been infected with HIV since the early 1980s, and that by the end of the century, between 30 million and 40 million people would have the virus. Two years earlier, Harvard's Global AIDS Policy Coalition had forecasted as many as 120 million HIV infections by the year 2000.

U.S. News & World Report estimates that the global dollar loss from AIDS by the turn of the century to be a "worst-case" scenario of $514 billion; a "best-case" scenario is $356 billion. The number of children orphaned worldwide could reach 3.7 million. In the United States alone, between $81 billion and $107 billion will be lost due to AIDS. Yet between 1986 and 1992, Congress appropriated only $168 million to the State Department's HIV/AIDS program, and funding for AIDS prevention decreased from $497 million in 1990 to $480 million in 1992.

And then in the summer of '92, the American medical establishment admitted there were people who have AIDS without having the HIV virus. AIDS had been defined since the early eighties by HIV; how could the government suddenly redefine it? Unless of course, the HIV virus is not the real cause of AIDS.

DUESBERG: HIV DOES NOT CAUSE AIDS

World-renowned Professor Peter Duesberg lost his prestige and government grants when he told the President's Commission on AIDS that the HIV virus could not cause AIDS. Dr. Duesberg specializes in molecular and cell biology and has published over 180 papers on the subject. He is credited with discovering cancer-causing retroviral oncogens, a genetic structure common to all retroviruses, including HIV. Yet because Duesberg believes that HIV is irrelevant to AIDS, the NIH rescinded his $350,000 cancer research grant.

According to Dr. Duesberg, AIDS is a syndrome of twenty-five old diseases including pneumonia, Kaposi's sarcoma, wasting syndrome, lymphoma, dementia, diarrhea, candidiasis, and tuberculosis. He believes AIDS in the U.S. and Europe is mostly caused by the consumption of psychoactive drugs that have continued to escalate since the Vietnam War; only a minority of AIDS cases are the result of clinical deficiencies.

Duesberg:

"The cause of AIDS is not sexual activity and associated viral and microbial infections, all of which we have learned to live with in the last three billion years of life. Natural and synthetic psychoactive drugs are the only new pathogens around since the 1970s, and the only new disease syndrome around is AIDS, and both are found in exactly the same populations."

Dr. Duesberg claims African AIDS is a series of old diseases — fever, diarrhea, tuberculosis, and slim disease—with a new name. It is precisely because AIDS is caused by protein malnutrition, parasitic infections, and poor sanitation that it is distributed randomly in Africa.

Duesberg proposes that the HIV virus is only a marker for AIDS. Since all viruses are primarily disease-causing before immunity, and *HIV is actively present in only one out of every 10,000 T-cells*, how could HIV cause AIDS as many as ten years later? The presence of antibodies to HIV and the absence of HIV symptoms is "classical evidence" that the body's immune system neutralizes HIV.

According to Dr. Duesberg, HIV is unproven as the cause of AIDS: There is *no conclusive evidence* that it replicates or destroys human cells in the body. When the actual virus can be found in a person who has been diagnosed with AIDS, its concentration is so low that special lab procedures have to be used to induce HIV to grow outside the body in order for HIV to be detectable. Duesberg contends that because HIV exists in so few cells, that even if it did destroy them, the result would be "like a pinprick."

Robert Root-Bernstein, Ph.D., Associate Professor of Physiology at Michigan State University, concurs:

"There is no longer any doubt that HIV is not necessary to cause immune deficiency. The question is whether the causes of HIV-free AIDS are also at work in people with HIV, and therefore what role HIV plays in causing AIDS in anyone."

Duesberg charges that those who challenge the HIV/AIDS hypothesis are ostracized because they have refused to "jump on the $3 billion HIV bandwagon." *The real reason the NIH revoked his $350,000 grant was because one of their "star scholars" accused them of wasting $3 billion on HIV research.*

Duesberg:

"Scientists researching AIDS are much less inclined to ask scrutinizing questions about the etiology of AIDS when they have invested huge sums of money in companies that make money on the hypothesis that HIV is the AIDS virus. William Haseltine and Max Essex, for example, who are two of the top five AIDS researchers in the country, have millions in stocks in a company they founded that has developed and will sell AIDS kits that test for HIV. How could they be objective? Gallo stands to make a lot of money from patent rights on the virus. His entire reputation depends on this virus. If HIV is not the cause of AIDS, there's nothing left for Gallo."

If there are still any doubts that censorship exists in the United States, consider this: "Good Morning America" flew Duesberg to New York City, booked him in a hotel, and the night before his scheduled appearance called to cancel due to "something urgent." The next morning Duesberg tuned in to the morning news show only to see his replacement, Dr. Anthony Fauci, espouse the government's line on AIDS. Similarly, scheduled interviews on "McNeil-Lehrer News Hour," CNN, and the Bay Area's Channel 2 News were all canceled, and two lengthy interviews with the *San Francisco Chronicle* were never published.

Professor Duesberg maintains that the HIV/AIDS theory is a "crutch," that slow viruses are offered when medicine does not know or does not want to know the real cause of a disease. On a color poster depicting the HIV virus, Professor Duesberg wrote:

First virus to kill without biochemical activity!
First virus to kill 50 to 100 percent of its carriers!
First virus to kill only after antiviral immunity!
First virus to be co-discovered a year after its discovery!

If there is a strong possibility that HIV does not cause AIDS, then why do so many scientists support the HIV theory? Duesberg explains:

"It's a selection process. The ones who agree HIV causes AIDS get their articles printed . . . Researchers are

like anybody else. They fight for their jobs, they're intimi-
dated, they don't stand up . . . AIDS has become an international business, an industry . . . It's very hard to talk to a
person who has a contract with a drug company in his pock-
et. How do you know that he's telling you the truth? Times
have changed. This is high-stakes science, financially."

Gary Bauer, head of President Reagan's Office of Policy
Development, was very disturbed when a White House meeting that
proposed to discuss HIV's role or non-role in AIDS was cancelled:
"People like Dr. Duesberg need to continue to have access to research
funds so that if we are heading in the wrong direction, that can be
proved."
Why isn't the NIH open to the possibility that the loss of
immune function could be due to extensive drug use or contaminated
vaccinations? Government authorities have never explained why
Duesberg is wrong; they've simply ignored or vilified his views.
Duesberg should be able to express his views freely in the establishment
press without censorship or fear of retaliation from the government and
medical establishment.

WHO DISCOVERED HIV - GALLO OR MONTAGNIER?

The U.S. government, medical research labs, and pharmaceuti-
cal companies all have vested interests in the HIV retrovirus theory. The
United States and France own the HIV patent. Every time someone is
tested for HIV, the U.S. federal government, the French government, Dr.
Robert Gallo and Dr. Luc Montagnier all receive money.
There has been much dispute over who really discovered HIV.
In April of 1984, the Reagan Administration named prominent research
scientist Dr. Robert Gallo the discoverer of the retrovirus responsible for
AIDS: "Today we have another miracle in the long honor roll of
American medicine and science," announced Health & Human Services
Secretary Margaret Heckler. The day before Gallo's crowning, the New
York Times quoted an official at the CDC as claiming that Dr. Luc
Montagnier's laboratory at the Pasteur Institute in France was the first to
isolate the AIDS virus. After three years of arguing, the U.S. and France
decided in 1987 to split the credit for the discovery of HIV and share the
royalties from the test. Five years later lawyers for the Pasteur Institute
sought to recover over $20 million that the U.S. government had earned
from the test.

Dr. Gallo, who has received about $100,000 a year from the HIV test, was investigated in the early 1990s by the NIH's Office of Scientific Integrity on charges of perjury and patent fraud. All evidence points to the fact that Gallo "stole" the discovery from the French. Montagnier and his team had published a report on HIV in May of 1983, and then sent a strain of the virus to Gallo at the National Institute of Cancer. Since the Gallo culture was identical to the French strain, Gallo's culture had to have come from Dr. Montagnier's lab.

In Gallo's 1984 science paper on HIV, Gallo's assistant, Dr. Mikulas Popovic, had tried to give credit to the French for discovering HIV. Dr. Gallo struck out Popovic's references to the French, writing in the margin, "Mika, are you crazy?" The NIH's Office of Scientific Integrity's principal investigator, Suzanne Hadley, found numerous false statements in Gallo's report, including several about the growth of the AIDS virus in the lab. Despite all of this evidence, the NIH cleared Gallo of any "wrong doing."

Perhaps senior officials at the NIH were aware in 1984 that Gallo's statements in his patent application were false. Did Gallo and the U.S. government accept the scientific glory and wealth that came with discovering the HIV virus to give the illusion that the Reagan administration was actually doing something about AIDS? If the top scientific researcher in the U.S. lacks credibility, then the government does as well. How can the federal government admit that a mistake was made, considering the billions of dollars spent on HIV?

THE "NEW AIDS VIRUS" - AIDS WITHOUT HIV

At the Eighth International Conference on AIDS in Amsterdam in July of 1992, scientists admitted to investigating numerous cases of patients who had AIDS-like conditions without being infected with HIV. The World Health Organization announced that AIDS would henceforth be referred to as "HIV Disease."

Many cases of HIV-free AIDS patients had been documented for several years, but it wasn't until the Amsterdam conference that the world media printed front page stories about the "new disease." In 1990 the prominent British medical journal, *The Lancet*, published an article which confirmed that many patients who were HIV-negative fulfilled all the criteria for AIDS as defined by the CDC and the WHO, including Kaposi's sarcoma (KS) and pneumocystis carinii pneumonia (PCP).

Most of the patients with the "new AIDS virus" had HIV risk factors such as needle sharing, unprotected sex, or a history of blood transfusions. Like AIDS, their T-4 white cell counts dropped and they developed potentially fatal opportunistic infections. Dr. Alvin

Friedman-Kien of the New York University Medical Center suggested that since gay men and IV drug users contracted infections such as gonorrhea, herpes, and hepatitis, these AIDS-like cases possibly reflected the immune-suppression effects of common germs or poor nutrition.

During the summer of 1992, the U.S. government claimed there were only sixty-eight cases of "AIDS without HIV"; Dr. Duesberg was aware of more than 3,000 cases. In a reply to Michael Mason's (the director of WHO's Global Program on AIDS) call "to launch a worldwide study of this situation as soon as possible," Duesberg wrote a letter (dated 25 September 1992) to the journal *Science*:

> "I am responding to this call with an offer to provide anyone who requests it a list of references to more than 800 HIV-free immunodeficiencies and AIDS-defining diseases in all major American and European AIDS risk groups. In addition, I can provide references to more than 2,200 HIV-free African AIDS cases that all meet the World Health Organization's definition of AIDS."

On 17 October 1992 a team of Japanese scientists wrote a similar letter to *The Lancet*:

> "The latest International Conference on AIDS in Amsterdam seems to have provoked dispute about the [cause] of the disease: Is AIDS truly caused by HIV? . . . The number of potential so-called HIV-negative cases seems to be increasing."

In their letter to *The Lancet*, the Japanese scientists reported that "blood samples were collected from 227 Ghanian AIDS patients diagnosed by WHO clinical criteria in Africa." Fifty-nine percent of the AIDS patients tested negative for HIV, though they had been clinically diagnosed by the WHO as having AIDS because of weight loss, prolonged diarrhea, dermatological diseases, and neurological disorders.

Duesberg:
> "One of the predictions of nonviral AIDS is that you would see HIV-free AIDS cases. The other is that you would see AIDS-free HIV cases. A study just came out in

The Lancet on a man who had been HIV-positive for ten years, but ten recipients of his blood are perfectly healthy."

The Lancet reported that people who are HIV-positive do not necessarily develop AIDS: Many adults and infants who have tested HIV-positive have failed to become ill even fourteen years after the original diagnosis. Michael Lange, M.D., an infectious disease specialist at St. Luke's Roosevelt Hospital in New York City, observed:

"We were all forced into a very dogmatic and simplistic view of what caused AIDS. Today I think even the greatest proponents of HIV no longer believe that it does all that damage to the immune system by itself. There have to be other factors involved. *And because of the HIV hypothesis, there's been little or no research done on what those other factors may be.*"

HEMOPHILIACS

Medical data suggests that HIV has no influence on the mortality of hemophiliacs; rather, it is the quality and purity of the blood clotting factor that seems to determine whether a hemophiliac will suffer immune suppression. About 15,000 of the 17,000 to 18,000 hemophiliacs in the U.S. are HIV–positive, and all were exposed between 1980 and 1985 through contaminated blood banks. As of June 1991, only 10 percent—1,535 cases of AIDS—had occurred among hemophiliacs in the U.S. The overwhelming majority who had been infected with HIV for eight or more years were apparently still free of AIDS.

If AIDS is a sexually transmitted disease caused by HIV, then logically the group engaging in the most sex should be the hardest hit. According to the Centers For Disease Control and Prevention, prostitutes do not even *constitute* an AIDS risk group. And of those prostitutes who are infected with HIV, most have abused intravenous drugs. Whether condoms can provide total protection is extremely doubtful, since the microscopic holes in condoms are big enough to allow penetration of HIV.

AIDS STATISTICS ARTIFICIALLY INFLATED

By 1 January 1993 the CDC's original definition of AIDS— HIV–positive with one of twenty-five diseases—was expanded to having HIV with either cancer of the cervix, bacterial pneumonia, or tuberculosis. As a consequence, the statistics of those with AIDS has been artificially inflated: From 250,000 in 1982, to 400,000 by January 1993. In its December 1992 issue, *The Lancet* published a study that attributed the huge increase in the number of women with a sudden AIDS diagnosis as the result (in large part) of having cervical cancer. According to the CDC, the top nine causes of death remained unchanged between 1987 and 1990, while the number of deaths from AIDS increased significantly during that period. AIDS mortality, which was the fifteenth leading cause of death in 1987, had moved up to tenth place by 1990, and to ninth place by 1993. AIDS acquired through heterosexual transmission had increased from 2 percent to 7 percent between 1985 and 1993.

In 1994 the WHO estimated that the number of AIDS cases worldwide had risen 60 percent, from 2.5 million in July 1993 to about 4 million in July of 1994—the total number of HIV-infected patients was estimated to be 17 million. Through the end of June 1994, the CDC announced it had received 401,749 reported cases of individuals with AIDS in the U.S., of whom 243,423 had died; ninety-two people *each day* were supposedly dying from AIDS-related diseases. The CDC claimed that in the previous eighteen months, 47 percent of new cases were among homosexual men, 28 percent among intravenous drug users, and 9 percent among heterosexuals who had contracted AIDS through sex.

Clearly a growing number of independent researchers believe that the HIV virus is not the sole cause of AIDS, that additional co-factors such as malnutrition, multiple infections, and/or drug abuse are required in order for AIDS to manifest. Even Dr. Luc Montagnier, the discoverer of the HIV virus, has come to the conclusion that HIV is "not a sufficient cause of AIDS on its own." Yet the "AIDS establishment" continues to concentrate most of its resources on HIV research. As Dr. Duesberg observed in the late 1980s, HIV is a billion dollar business.

CHAPTER TEN

POLITICAL AGENDAS

There has never been a time before this when medical research and basic biological research were both connected to the money machine. The fundamental change is that now biology is a for-profit science. Yearly, the directory of biotechnology companies grow.

Professor Peter Duesberg
Molecular Biologist
University of California, Berkeley

THE "AIDS ESTABLISHMENT"

Those who are a part of the "AIDS establishment" adhere to the "official line"—that HIV causes AIDS. These are the people who receive all the grant money, are on the boards of all the AIDS fundraising organizations, and have their AIDS articles published in the establishment's scientific journals. Newspapers and television networks report the establishment findings, rarely making judgements on the accuracy of information taken directly from press representatives at public health agencies. If a major newspaper or television network dares to question the "AIDS research establishment," upper management and/or ownership almost always suppresses it. On the few occasions when a newspaper prints a contradictory viewpoint, the article is usually buried on the back page of the Sports or Classified Section and public reaction is negligible.

THE FEDERAL GOVERNMENT FAILS TO PRODUCE A TREATMENT FOR AIDS

On 7 November 1991 when Earvin "Magic" Johnson announced his retirement from professional basketball—"Because of the HIV virus that I have attained, I will have to retire from the Lakers"—fear over the escalation of heterosexual transmission increased. Forty-eight hours after Johnson's announcement, the CDC reported 40,000 requests for AIDS testing: phones rang off the hook at AIDS clinics throughout the country; stocks in condom companies increased in value on the New York Stock Exchange. The Sunday after Johnson's retirement, Dr. Anthony Fauci, director of NIAID, was interviewed on "This Week With David Brinkley": "We may not have a cure [by the end of this decade], but I am confident that with a combination of drugs, we will be able to prolong the disease-free state."

By now most people had lost confidence in Fauci's leadership. Since 1983, desperate AIDS victims had been circumventing FDA rules and importing foreign drugs. A huge medical underground of alternative medicine and unapproved drugs developed as a direct consequence of AIDS, and groups such as Act Up in New York City and Project Inform in San Francisco began exerting enormous pressure on the American medical establishment to overhaul the system. In 1985 Fauci had convinced Congress to allot more money for AIDS research so that NIAID could begin clinical drug trials. By 1987 the federal government's multi-million dollar research effort had still not produced one treatment for AIDS. AIDS activists were particularly incensed when Fauci refused to advise doctors about aerosol pentamidine, a treatment that prolonged the lives of AIDS patients suffering from PCP (pneumocystis carinii pneumonia). Small private companies distributed information about aerosol pentamidine, while Fauci stood back and did nothing. In 1988 the director of NIAID told Congress that he wouldn't follow his own government's guidelines if he had AIDS.

AZT IS APPROVED

The FDA approved its first drug for AIDS patients, AZT, in March of 1987. Although it has a number of detrimental side effects, AZT was nevertheless rushed through the FDA's drug approval process. *Burroughs Wellcome's President of Research, David Barry, made a behind-the-scenes deal with the FDA (which he had worked for in the 1970s), managing to bypass government bureaucracy to get FDA approval.* AZT has been shown to produce a short term (months) increase in T-cell population, but this is invariably followed by a rapid decline to a point lower than before treatment. AZT's toxicity causes nausea, diarrhea, and headaches. Conflicts of interest—scientists who have based their careers on AZT and/or have financial dealings with Burroughs Wellcome—dominate the government's clinical trial system. As Bruce Nussbaum depicted in his illuminating book, *Good Intentions*: "PIs [professional investigators] test drugs by private pharmaceutical companies for personal gain, for money that goes to their universities, and for power."

With its seventeen institutes and six scientific centers, the National Institutes of Health in Bethesda, Maryland is the center of medical research in the U.S. (By 1994 its annual budget was $11 billion.) Three-quarters of the $9 billion the NIH received from Congress in 1991 for medical research was sent to professional investigators. Although hundreds of millions of dollars have been spent on AIDS drug trials, drugs that are much more beneficial than AZT have not been tested. PIs have their own agenda, and their misuse of power is the result of a lack of accountability. The drug choice of the AIDS underground, AL 721—a safe food substance with antiviral properties—never made it through the FDA's bureaucracy because its sponsors didn't have the right connections. When AL 721 came up for FDA review in early 1987, PIs voted it a "low priority" since their careers were tied to AZT. Anthony Fauci ordered a small clinical trial to "debunk" AL 721 and by 1988 it was dead.

Small companies do not have the political connections and resources to compete with the big pharmaceutical companies in the FDA's drug development program. There were at least six other drugs less toxic than AZT that had a fate similar to AL 721. Because Burroughs Wellcome had political clout and knew how to operate within the system, it could cut through administrative delays and go directly to FDA advisory committees. *In AZT's first year of sales, Burroughs Wellcome made $200 million in profits.*

From 1982 until the spring of 1993, AZT was the premier drug and standard therapy for HIV infection and AIDS—*80 percent of all federal drug trials involved AZT.* By 1989 the NIH was recommending AZT for people HIV-positive but healthy, after studies supposedly indicated that AZT could stave off the onset of AIDS. Burroughs Wellcome's ads claimed that AZT would "put time on your side." This recommendation pushed the number of potential AZT users from 40,000 to more than half a million. The first major independent study, published by Dr. John Hamilton of the Veterans Administration, found that there was "no statistical difference in progression to AIDS" between the AZT group and the placebo group. In February of 1992, the *New England Journal of Medicine* published the first study that compared patients receiving early

AZT treatment to those who waited to take AZT until they developed AIDS symptoms. Researchers found that AZT's benefits run out after twelve to eighteen months and that early treatment does not extend people's lives. In fact, after eighteen months on AZT, the rate of death skyrockets.

Even more devastating were the results from a four-year Anglo-French study which examined AZT in depth. The "Concorde" study found that those who began taking AZT while symptom-free died sooner than those who were healthy yet HIV-positive and received no treatment at all.[19] *Asymptomatics comprised 38 percent of Burroughs Wellcome's market for AZT.*

As a chemotherapy drug, AZT kills cells indiscriminately, attacking the bone marrow, which is where cells of the immune system are made.

Duesberg:
"AZT is simply stopping the growth of DNA. AZT is hell for the bone marrow. It is poison. . . AZT produces what is called AIDS. It attacks the center of the immune system. It is killing people."

Molecular biologist Harvey Bialy, research editor of *Bio/Technology*, agrees: "The administration of AZT, as a treatment for AIDS, amounts to introgenic genocide."

And what about the costs? In 1987 a year's supply of AZT retailed for $10,000. Due to pressure from Congress, Burroughs Wellcome lowered their price to $6,200 in 1989; by the summer of 1992, AZT cost $3,159 a year, a third of its original price. (As AZT decreased in cost, Burroughs Wellcome raised the amount of its largest selling drug, another AIDS drug called Zovirax.) AZT has not saved one person; it may actually shorten lives. Despite these facts, physicians who treat AIDS patients are still being trained to prescribe AZT, to adhere to the "AIDS establishment."

In an effort to restore some of AZT's merit, a panel of independent experts have suggested that AZT be administered to pregnant women who are HIV-positive and still healthy, and to their babies during the first six weeks after birth. These so-called experts have taken preliminary data from an early 1990s study and concluded that only 8 percent of AZT babies had contracted HIV, versus 25 percent in the placebo

[19] The "Concorde" study was published in *The Lancet* in April of 1994.

group. There is no solid data on long-term effects of AZT on pregnant women without AIDS symptoms or on children who receive AZT in utero—the only solid data on AZT is that it has not saved lives or prevented the progression of AIDS. Yet we have the Los Angeles County Board of Supervisors considering widespread HIV testing of pregnant women; they are even seeking a legal opinion as to whether county health facilities can force women at high risk for AIDS to be tested and forced to take AZT. Due to the AIDS establishment's propaganda, pregnant HIV-positive women are beginning to believe that their babies will possibly die if they don't take AZT.

After over a decade of research and the investment of millions of dollars, the four drugs currently approved by the FDA to treat AIDS are all toxic and ineffective, exacerbating the disease. AZT, ddI (dideoxynosine), ddC (dideoxycytidine), and D4T (stavudine) do not prolong life. Each of these drugs is designed to stop viral replication, but in the process, destroy healthy cells. In the spring of 1995, researchers for the AIDS establishment were experimenting with a "drug cocktail," which they claimed could provide a "potent antiviral punch against HIV" to slow the progression of the disease. More propaganda.

At the Tenth International AIDS Conference in Yokohama, Japan in 1994, 10,000 researchers concluded that a cure for AIDS was nowhere in sight. Because the pace of AIDS research was so slow, researchers decided that after 1994 the annual AIDS conference would be held every other year. Dr. George Lundberg, Editor of the *Journal of the American Medical Association*, predicted that "no successful method of treatment or prevention will have been fully implemented" by the end of the century and that "AIDS will still be a serious endemic disease throughout the world."

EPILOGUE

The doctor of the future will give no medicine, but will interest his patients in the care of the human frame, in diet, and in the cause and prevention of disease.

Thomas Edison

For over a decade, Randy Koppang and Harvey Brennan have suffered from opportunistic infections associated with AIDS. Today both men consider their good health a direct result of nutritional and alternative therapies.

Randy Koppang:

"I feel it of greatest importance to begin with an affirmation. The most valuable statement such a book as this can make is that total healing is readily possible!

"I make a substantial distinction between healing and curing. I believe healing implies something more than a relief of symptoms, that the patient has accepted responsibility to remove illness from his life. Diseases as tenacious as cancer and

AIDS can be totally healed if the patient changes his lifestyle accordingly.

"My basic complaint has been chronic systemic candidiasis. The problems I had were protein malnutrition, oedema, pneumonia, amoebas, parasites, and chronic yeast infection. Had my diagnosis occurred now, due to the ever encompassing Center For Disease Control set of AIDS symptomology—I probably would have been diagnosed as having AIDS symptoms. I did have AIDS! But I did not have HIV! I suggest it wise to keep this in mind.

"Upon partial recovery and failing to re-establish a sensible diet, I (unknowingly) began to contract a seriously chronic yeast infection. I had this problem for years prior to receiving an accurate diagnosis. The symptoms began as random patches of pimply skin rash. These enlarged into "weepy" open sores that wouldn't heal. At my most acute state, I had severe chronic fatigue, bad digestion, gas, severe skin rashes all over my body, and allergic reaction to virtually all forms of carbohydrate foods. Early on I recognized the causal relationship between my allergic food response and flare-ups in the skin rash. But it was about five years before I discovered that my condition was not food allergy per se. Rather, I had an opportunistic infection, which, then being out of control, inflamed like gasoline on a fire whenever I ate certain foods.

"I visited numerous physicians and got little relief. Most often I was told I had eczema and was given cortisone, which made me worse. This disease plagued me for about fifteen years. I've been working on my recovery for ten of those years. My recovery was first and foremost nutritionally focused:

1. Keeping a dietary journal—recording the order of a greatly varied rotation diet. This single approach afforded me the *most* substantial relief!

2.   Abstinence from all forms of sugar, including all fruits, fresh and especially dried.

3.   Supplementation with vitamins and minerals; natural or herbal antibiotics; digestive enzymes.

4.   Oxygen   therapies: H_2O_2, Homozone, stabilized electrolytes of oxygen.

5.   Systematic detoxification: I'm sure my recovery may have been more rapid had I the time and funds to partake in an extended stay at one of the alternative health clinics located in Mexico. Given this as unaffordable, I listened to many lectures offered by the practitioners who run those clinics (numbering about thirty now), and applied their nutritional and detoxification experience to my own.

"Currently, I have very nearly returned to what most people take for granted as "normal": during a long, drawn-out state of illness one becomes conditioned to that state; one forgets what "normal" health is like. Virtually all of my symptoms now have been healed. An exception is an impairment due to the candida having infected my eyes.

"It goes without saying that the most fundamental element of my strategy for recovery was the determination to take responsibility for oneself and do it!"

Harvey Brennan:

"The product *True Health* has confirmed for me—I'm about ready to say I'm almost totally convinced—that if I would take care of my body properly, I probably would not experience disease to any serious degree. I have a long history of experience that has brought me to this point. And *True Health*, which I have taken for almost four years, is the cap on the bottle.

"As a child I was asthmatic and had allergies, flu, and colds regularly. All I ever knew to take for them were antibiotics. Today I know that these medications debilitated my immune system.

"I had this severe asthma attack while doing disaster relief work for the government, and an attorney (who had asthma) told me that he could cure my asthma without any drugs, that all I had to do was try his diet. I was so sick, so depressed, I thought—why not? He put me on a low-fat, high-carbohydrate, medium-protein diet. Within a week I was better, and as long as I stayed on that diet, I never had asthma again. I found out I was allergic to milk and sugar. He told me that asthma was nothing more than hypoglycemia of one form, that it was the opposite of diabetes. It's a blood sugar imbalance, that's all it is. Doctors had never told me that; I went to all kinds of doctors and suffered so much. It's so simple and they never knew it.

"Being the human that I am, I went back to my old ways, and I noticed that when I did allow my body to deteriorate, I'd promptly get asthma and other illnesses. Being so addicted to food, I would go sin by eating all of this crummy food, until I was dying, and then I would go on a diet. At least it did teach me that there was an alternative method to health. I read more books about health and learned about fasting.

"When I went through my divorce I experienced real health problems. I hated myself for the divorce—a lot of self abuse, and I nearly became an alcoholic, a sex addict—I just went through all kinds of strange behaviors in an effort to avoid the pain. I smoked a lot and drank a lot and screwed around a lot more than I should have. I was living in New York. I got sick. I'd go to doctors and get bombarded with antibiotics. I got to the point where I couldn't even walk one block without total exhaustion. I got phlebitis, pink eye, hepatitis, a venereal disease, flu, colds. All they did was treat me with antibiotics. And of course, because my diet was bad and my lifestyle bad, my body's metabolism was totally screwed up. After every illness I got worse—total exhaustion after two flights of stairs, two blocks of walking. I thought I was dying. In about 1980-81, I was diagnosed as having contracted a disease which we couldn't identify (this was before HIV).

"I could have decided to die—I was that sick—but I didn't because of my children. I thought it was the ultimate travesty to die due to my personal irresponsibility. An alternative doctor told me I had to clean up my life; no more screwing around; take vitamin supplements; fast so that the body can clean itself, purge itself—animals don't eat when they are sick but we keep feeding ourselves. I started going to chiropractors since regular medicine—drugs and antibiotics—destroy my immune system. I started taking herbs because of this doctor. So up until I heard of *True Health*, I maintained my health through herbal and vitamin therapy, proper diet, fasting, and going to chiropractors.

"Eight years after the New York treatment, I began to notice that my metabolism was slipping again. (In 1989 I had the HIV test and it came out positive.) My T-4 count had deteriorated; I kept slipping—480, 450, 420. I saw what AZT does, and I didn't want to go that route. I tried aloe vera, which was expensive and didn't do a bit of good. And then, through a friend, I heard of *True Health*.

"Ever since I started taking *True Health*, all kinds of wonderful things have happened. My body had been deteriorating—all the bad symptoms had been coming back. But since I started taking this True Health product, everything has arrested and my metabolism is getting better. I was never able to eat ice cream without an allergic reaction. And now I can have a chocolate shake, hamburgers and fries, and I do not catch colds or the flu as long as I take this stuff. Before I was sick all of the time; if it wasn't colds or flu, it was allergies. *True Health* has really been great. My fatigue has gone. My body has filled out. My skin is a lot healthier—I have color that I didn't have before. I was starting to look like an AIDS patient, real gaunt—you know how their skin looks kind of dead. And I've quit taking my vitamin therapies and all that other stuff. This is by far cheaper than all of the other stuff I've gone through. And my T-4 count is stable. I'm just so pleased with this product. I'm trying to get all my friends who are sick to try it.

"I visited an AIDS patient who had been in and out of coma, four or five times. He was literally skin and bones, had ghastly grey skin, and his family was feeding him hamburgers and french fries. I got him on the powder [*True Health*], off of all hospital food, and he got up and left the hospital in one week. After two weeks he filled out. He was taking other drugs, but this change was just absolutely incredible. When his doctor asked him what he was taking, the doctor told him to quit taking it and he died—he rapidly deteriorated after going off the powder and capsules [essential fatty acid]. Now I'm not saying he wouldn't have died with the powder, but it's a fact that as soon as he stopped taking it he died. I'm really convinced *True Health* does a lot of good.

"My roommate is HIV–positive, too. He had been ridiculing me for taking *True Health*, for spending the money. But when his T-4 count dropped dramatically—from 800 to 600 to 400 in just a few months time—he started taking the *True Health* and his T-4 count went from 425 to 519 in a month and a half. Again, I can't say this product does this, but we see an example of someone benefiting from the product.

"I know it has helped me. I've got my family on it. My dad is on it. I know that people can live long and have a good quality of life if they would change their lifestyles."

Americans are increasingly opting for alternative health care practices. The average person choosing alternative therapy is well educated, financially stable, and enjoying good health. Americans are now spending $40 billion a year on alternative treatments, compared to $10 billion in 1987. According to a recent FDA survey, 35 percent of the population use some form of alternative medicine, while 25 percent use alternative medicine exclusively. In January 1993, the *New England Journal of Medicine* published a study confirming that one-third of all Americans regularly turn to nonconventional medicine administered by chiropractors, acupuncturists, homeopaths, masseuses, and meditation teachers—all of whom have been labeled in the past as "quacks" by the AMA.

Due to increased public pressure, the NIH organized an Office of Alternative Medicine (OAM) in 1992. But until there is legitimate proof, we must not be fooled into thinking the medical bureaucracy is changing its ways. Only $2 million (covering about ten projects) of the NIH's overall 1993 budget of $10.3 billion was allotted for the study of alternative treatments. The research budget for 1994 was $3.5 million. An ex-NIH employee offered his opinion: "The NIH director's office has set up the OAM in such a way that few projects of interest will be proposed and even fewer funded. In a few years, the NIH will give up, saying 'we tried, and there's nothing there.'"

It is the behind-the-scenes political pressure from the medical autocracy that urges Congress to maintain the status quo. According to a *Boston Globe* analysis of Federal Election Commission records, PAC contributors to Capitol Hill leaders and lawmakers increased by 61 percent in 1992 (an election year), for a total of $1.9 million. The AMA— America's leading health PAC—gave Republican Senator Robert Packwood $238,808 in direct and indirect contributions. Senator Packwood supported moderate health care reform. Whereas Representative Les Aucoin, Packwood's 1992 campaign opponent, supported a national health care system and did not receive one financial contribution from the AMA. Packwood defeated Aucoin by a narrow margin. Congressman Henry Waxman, a fervent supporter of increased

FDA enforcement powers, received $356,000 in PAC money from med-
ical, pharmaceutical, and insurance companies.

"Whatever the Party holds to be truth is truth," warned Orwell.
If you are a threat to the establishment, they will do anything to destroy
your credibility. Not once during True Health's dealings with the FDA
did a government official accuse them of having an inferior product.[20]
The FDA was created to ensure the safety of prescription drugs, not to
deny Americans access to natural therapies.

Since the early 1960s, the medical establishment has attempted
to classify vitamins and nutrients as prescription drugs, to force people
to pay for a physician's visit to obtain a prescription, *to control people's
health*. Nutritional deficiencies, which trigger most chronic diseases,
have escalated the cost of health care in America to unaffordable
heights—it is criminal not to have physician education in nutritional biochemistry.

The United States medical monopoly could not exist without the
enforcement powers of the Food and Drug Administration. Americans
must take back control of their health care before it is too late. Congress
must *permanently* remove vitamins and nutritional supplements from
the authority of the FDA, perhaps by establishing a federal nutrition
agency with independent status—one that includes representation from
universities, citizen health groups, and manufacturers. As long as the
FDA is allowed to manipulate the law through its power and influence,
every American's fundamental right to choose their own health care will
be in jeopardy.

---

[20]The FDA continues to monitor True Health: FDA Investigator Dallas
Galbraith issued a Notice of Inspection to Richard Stokley on 28
November 1994.

APPENDIX A

THE BENEFITS OF NUTRITION

If most health problems were diet-related and could be either modified or avoided with improved nutrition, imagine what the implications would be. *Benefits From Human Nutrition Research*, a 1971 Department of Agriculture study, determined that the solution to major illness could, indeed, be found in nutrition: "Better health, a longer active lifespan, and greater satisfaction from work, family and leisure time are among the benefits to be obtained from improved diets and nutrition . . . One purpose of this study is to conduct an evaluative analysis of current problems related to human nutrition and to present the results of this analysis in a meaningful manner that will facilitate policy decisions about future programs of research on food and human nutrition topics." Unfortunately, most Americans are not aware of *Benefits From Human Nutrition Research* since the study was not made available to the public.[21] Thirty million dollars was allocated to this nutritional research project, yet taxpayers were not told the results. Twenty-four years later, the federal government is still concealing the truth.

"The greatest homage we can pay to truth is to use it," observed Ralph Waldo Emerson. Accurate information is essential in a democracy. When the public is misled with false information, making rational

---

[21] See Appendix B.

decisions becomes impossible. Given the choice, who wouldn't prefer a nutritional supplement to prescription drugs with side effects, or even major surgery? Vitamins, minerals, and nutrients such as essential fatty acids can play a major role in *preventing* illnesses as serious as heart disease and cancer, as well as chronic illnesses such as arthritis and diabetes. But if nutrition was really the answer to most health problems, why hasn't the government promoted it? Billions of dollars and countless lives could have been saved since the Department of Agriculture's 1971 study. There is, however, a lot more money to be made in continued medical treatment and drugs than there is in vitamins and herbs. That is the disturbing truth.

THE U.S. HEALTH CARE SYSTEM

The United States health care system is among the most expensive and least efficient of the twenty-four industrialized countries in Europe and North America, ranking seventeenth in life expectancy and twentieth in the prevention of infant mortality. Medical costs have soared from $75 billion in 1970 to over $942.5 billion in 1993, with projections of $1,060.5 trillion for 1994 (15 percent of the gross national product—GNP). In 1993, the annual health cost per capita in the U.S. was $3,358, twice as much as Canada's and four times the amount spent in Britain. The United States spends more per capita and a greater proportion of its GNP on medical costs than any other nation.

TOTAL U.S. SPENDING ON HEALTH CARE

DOLLARS IN BILLIONS

1975	$132
1980	$249
1985	$420
1990	$675
1991	$752
1992	$838.5
1993	$942.5
1994	$1,060.5 (15% of GNP)

PROJECTIONS IN TRILLIONS

1995	$1.073
2000	$1.6
2003	$2.0 (18% of GNP)

PER CAPITA SPENDING

1980	$1,000
1985	$1,710
1987	$2,000
1992	$3,160
1993	$3,358
2003	$7,059

Source: Office of the Actuary from the Health Care
            Financing Administration; Congressional Research
            Service Health Care Costs

Administrative overhead in the U.S. accounts for 22 percent of medical expenses, and malpractice suits have forced doctors to buy expensive insurance with the cost passed on to patients. Without health care reform, the Department of Commerce forecasts that health care expenditures will "rise by an annual rate of growth of 13.5 percent" in the next five years: By the year 2003, 20 percent of the GNP—$2 trillion—will be spent on health care, $7,059 per capita.

Fifty million Americans have inadequate medical insurance and 37 million are without coverage entirely. A 1992 University of Arkansas research study showed that one-half to two-thirds of hospitalized or institutionalized elderly Americans are malnourished. Of the 30 million over age sixty-five, 1 million are malnourished and 6 million are at high risk of malnutrition. The elderly are often forced to choose between food and medicine; medicine usually wins out. And the situation can only get worse. The over sixty-five population is expected to rise to an estimated 52 million by the year 2022.

The standard practice in this country is to treat an illness rather than prevent it from developing. Drugs are regularly prescribed without sufficient understanding or justification, and surgery is often performed when less riskier procedures are warranted. In 1992, only 3 to 5 percent of U.S. health care expenditures was spent on disease prevention.

In this age of technological innovation, the two leading causes of death—heart disease and cancer—continue to skyrocket. Instead of attacking the underlying cause of heart disease, doctors are trained to perform bypass surgery and angioplasty. Studies on bypass surgery have never justified its widespread use, yet it has been performed regardless of expense or risk. In the majority of angioplasties, the blockages recur.

Instead of allotting money towards the prevention of cancer, the medical establishment prescribes chemotherapy and radiation. The American Cancer Society hands out pamphlets telling us not to take Vitamin C supplements because of potential toxicity. Vitamin C—a water soluble nutrient—toxic! Toxicity symptoms rarely occur even with high doses of Vitamin C since the body eliminates any excess of ascorbic acid in the urine and through perspiration. In a 1993 article in the *Cancer Journal for Clinicians*, the American Cancer Society recommended that nutritional cancer cures be avoided: ". . . Some [of the approaches] involve potentially toxic doses of vitamins and/or other substances. Some are quite expensive. All pose the risk that patients who use them will abandon effective treatment." Yet, the American Cancer Society does not hesitate to endorse toxic, expensive, and potentially cancer-causing chemotherapy and radiation "therapies."

The cancer establishment, which includes the National Cancer Institute (NCI), the American Cancer Society, and the various foundations and pharmaceutical companies, have emphasized medical technology at the expense of prevention. Despite the billions of dollars spent on cancer research, and the American Cancer Society's claims that we are "winning the war on cancer," the reality is that the 5-year cure rate has not changed significantly in thirty years. Since the "war on cancer" was launched in 1971, the incidence of cancer has risen 18 percent and the death rate 7 percent; in September of 1994, Congress asked an independent panel of experts to evaluate why cancer is still on the rise after $23 billion in spending since 1971. According to the journal *Science*, "Overall death rates from many common cancers remain stubbornly unchanged—or even higher—than when the war began." At a press conference in Washington D.C., Dr. Samuel Epstein, a specialist in occupational and environmental medicine, explained: "The cancer establishment confuses the public with repeated claims that we are winning the war...Our ability to treat and cure most cancers has not materially improved." According to Dr. Epstein, "There are no accurate figures on cancer's overall cost. The best estimate is more than $100 billion a year. Where does it all go?"

Breast cancer is four times more common in the U.S. than in Japan. The typical American diet averages 40 percent of its calories from fat, while the traditional Japanese diet averages only 15 percent fat. If breast cancer could be reduced through eating less fat by just 10 percent, approximately 18,000 cases would be prevented annually, a savings of $177 million a year. Despite these statistics, the NCI cancelled a proposed Women's Health Trial that would have explored dietary fat in relation to cancer: Clinicians and researchers argued that the $10 million a year for the trial should be allocated for *detection and treatment* rather than *prevention*.

In 1969, the federal government dismissed the suggestion of nutrition experts, who urged the federal government to establish a federal nutrition agency with independent status.[22] Dr. Philip Lee, former HEW Assistant Secretary for Health, observed that "little or no attention has been paid to the nutritional health of the population" and that nutrition was treated as the "stepchild of food and agricultural policy." Agreeing with Lee's assessment, Congress' Office of Technology Assessment declared in 1978 that the federal government had not directed nutrition research "to deal with the changing health problems of the

---

[22] President Jean Mayer of Tufts University; Kenneth Schlossberg, Staff Director of the Senate Committee on Nutrition & Human Needs; and Dr. Artemis Simopoulos, Chairman of the Nutrition Coordinating Committee of the National Institutes of Health, recommended the establishment of a federal nutrition agency at the 1969 White House Conference on Food, Nutrition & Health.

American people."

Orthodox medicine has perpetuated the myth that our nutrition-al needs can be met by eating a "balanced diet." In 1974, the FDA assert-ed that vitamins "do not provide energy, nor do they construct or build any part of the body. . . Vitamins will not provide extra pep, vitality beyond normal expectations, or an unusual level of well being." In 1976, the AMA stated that "all the recommended nutrient intakes considered essential to maintenance of health in normal individuals can be provid-ed by a balanced diet of commercial foods including enriched and forti-fied items." *Where is the evidence to prove that diet alone can supply enough nutrients to attain an above-adequate level of health?* In many cases, a dietary supplement is beneficial precisely because it supplies a particular nutri-ent in a potency much higher than that which is found in food.

We have reached a time when the scientific evidence supporting the preventive and therapeutic use of vitamins, minerals, and other food factors is literally overwhelming. Although clinical trials, biochemical analyses, and epidemiological studies demonstrate how diet plays a major role in disease, the federal government has continually disregard-ed the importance of nutrition.

Recent studies on folic acid demonstrate how deceptive the RDAs are. While the official guidelines recommend 180 to 200 micro-grams of folic acid, clinical trials indicate that women of childbearing age need 400 to 800 micrograms a day during the first six weeks of preg-nancy to ensure against certain birth defects. Lower intakes of folic acid have been linked to spina bifida (paralysis, lifelong bowel and bladder problems) and anencephaly (which causes death just hours after birth). In *Benefits From Human Nutrition Research*, the Department of Agriculture determined that folic acid deficiency was a serious problem in the U.S. How many birth defects and deaths have occurred over the past twenty-five years as a consequence of the federal government's fail-ure to inform the public?

A lack of antioxidants—Vitamins C, E, and beta carotene (a form of vitamin A)—have been implicated in sixty age-related afflictions, including cancer and heart disease. In 1992, Dr. Gladys Block (University of California, Berkeley) published a review of twenty studies that monitored the incidence of mouth, throat, and stomach cancers in relation to Vitamin C intake: Those consuming the lowest intakes of Vitamin C were stricken at twice the rate of those consuming the most. Similarly, in more than twenty studies conducted at the National Cancer Institute, high levels of Vitamin C were linked to low rates of lung can-cer, cancers of the mouth, throat, stomach, bladder, and rectum. A University of Toronto study reported on a control group with bladder cancer that took high daily doses of Vitamin A (40,000 US), B_6 (100 mg), C (2,000 mg) and E (400 IU): They had 40 percent fewer tumors and lived twice as long as the control group that didn't take vitamins. Researchers at UCLA recently analyzed a ten-year federal health survey, reporting that low Vitamin C intake was a strong predictor of death from heart disease: Men who consumed 300 milligrams daily (five times the RDA) suffered 40 percent fewer deaths than those consuming 50 milligrams. Researchers at Harvard are seeing similar results with beta carotene and its relation to cardiovascular disease.

A search of Medlars' Data Base at the National Library of Medicine shows that since 1966, there have been more than 75,000 studies on nutrients that provide evidence of the health benefits of dietary supplements.

Yet not only does the government and mainstream medicine refuse to admit we should be taking nutritional supplements, *they intentionally mislead Americans with inaccurate information*. The 14 April 1994 issue of the *New England Journal of Medicine* published a study that evaluated the effects of antioxidants on 29,000 Finnish men who had smoked a pack of cigarettes a day for an average of thirty-six years. This joint effort of the U.S. National Cancer Institute and the Finnish National Public Institute—which cost $40 million—was designed to test the effectiveness of *low dosages* of Vitamin E and beta carotene on cigarette smokers. The results indicated that neither Vitamin E nor beta carotene by themselves or in combination reduced the incidence of lung cancer. One group that took beta carotene actually had a higher rate of lung cancer than the group taking a placebo.

The Finnish study simply defies common sense—no one ever claimed that vitamin supplementation could negate decades of moderate to heavy smoking. Furthermore, the study was too short in duration (five years), employed too low a dosage and/or utilized a population at too high a risk to demonstrate the beneficial effects of antioxidants. Although beta carotene has a history of safety in thousands of clinical trials, the networks (ABC, NBC, CBS, CNN) warned that, as a result of the Finnish study, antioxidants could be dangerous if taken as a dietary supplement. The *New York Times* entitled its front page article on the Finnish study, "Vitamin Supplements Are Seen As No Guard Against Diseases." Once again following the "official line," the media disregarded the multitude of studies that demonstrate the benefits of antioxidants used in optimum amounts. In their effort to mislead the public about nutrition, the government wasted $40 million of taxpayers' money on a study that should never have been undertaken in the first place.

BENEFITS FROM HUMAN NUTRITION RESEARCH —
A $30 MILLION GOVERNMENT STUDY

The 1990s health care crisis may have been averted if Americans had been told in 1971 about the Department of Agriculture's *Benefits From Human Nutrition Research* study. In 1970, health care in the United States accounted for $67.2 billion, 7 percent of the GNP; death rates for most illnesses were higher in the United States than in other countries of comparable economic development. In 1993, health care accounted for 14 percent of the GNP, and death rates still remained higher than in other industrialized countries.

Twenty-four years ago, the potential long-term benefits from nutritional research seemed endless. The Department of Agriculture's study concluded that the alleviation of nutrition-related health problems would result in "a vast reservoir of health and economical benefits." Each age, sex, ethnic, economic, and geographic segment of the population would prosper, with the lower economic groups improving most of all.

In 1971, the extent to which diet was believed to be involved in the development of disease was based mostly on the knowledge of abnormal metabolic pathways, developed by people who were already in advanced stages of illness; there was little knowledge about how and why normal metabolic changes took place. Nutritionists understood that the ultimate result of nutrition deficiency could sometimes take years before becoming apparent, as when a metabolite such as cholesterol accumulates. If an early adjustment in diet could prevent the development of blocked arteries later in life, what other diseases that occur later in old age could be avoided by a change in diet at a young age?

Researchers observed that even the small advances in nutritional knowledge greatly contributed to the reduction in the number of infant and maternal deaths, in the number of deaths from infectious diseases (especially among children), and in extending the productive life span and life expectancy. Improved nutrition is preventive medicine in that it can defer, or at least modify, the development of a disease state.

In *Benefits From Human Nutrition Research*, regional differences in the incidence of health problems—variations in the type and length of illnesses throughout the United States—were considered to be a reflection of the cumulative effect of low nutrient intake levels throughout the lifespan and by successive generations. For instance, pellagra, which occurs as the consequence of a niacin deficiency, had occurred in epidemic proportions in some of the southern states earlier in the century, when corn was the major protein source for low income families.

Also believed to be directly attributable to differences in the nutrient content of food were the geographic variances in death rates.

The highest death rate areas usually corresponded to those areas recognized by agriculturists to have depleted soil. Researchers noted that people who moved from a high death rate area to a low death rate area almost always increased their lifespan, while those who moved from a low death rate area into a higher rated area lost this advantage—proof of a relationship between chronic nutrient-deficient diets and the health of succeeding generations.

The potential benefits from improved nutrition, as indicated in *Benefits From Human Nutrition Research*, were significant:

HEALTH PROBLEM	POTENTIAL SAVINGS FROM IMPROVED DIET
Heart and Vasculatory	25% reduction in incidents 20% reduction in cost
Respiratory and Infectious	20% fewer incidents 15-20% fewer days lost $1 million reduction in medical $20 million reduction in cold remedies and tissues
Mental Health	10% fewer disabilities
Infant Mortality and Reproduction	50% fewer deaths 3 million fewer birth defects
Early Aging and Lifespan	10% improvement in chronic impairments
Arthritis	50% reduction in incidence 50% decrease in sick days 25% increase in employment $900 million saved per year
Dental Health	50% reduction in incidence, severity and expenditures
Diabetes and Carbohydrate Disorders	50% of cases avoided or improved
Osteoporosis	75% reduction in incidence
Obesity	80% reduction in incidence
Alcoholism	33% reduction in incidence 33% reduction in deaths caused by alcohol; 33% reduction in costs due to absenteeism, lowered production, accidents

HEALTH PROBLEM	POTENTIAL SAVINGS FROM IMPROVED DIET
Eyesight	20% fewer people blind or with corrective lenses
Allergies	20% reduction in incidence 90% reduction in milk and gluten allergic incidents
Digestive	25% fewer acute conditions 25% reduction in costs
Kidney and Urinary	20% reduction in deaths and acute conditions
Muscular Disorders	10% reduction in cases
Cancer	20% reduction in incidence and deaths
Improved Work	.5% increase in on-the-job efficiency productivity
Improved Growth and Development	25% fewer deaths and work days lost
Improved Learning Ability	Raise I.Q. by 10 points for persons with I.Q. 70-80

In *Benefits From Human Nutrition Research*, researchers determined that the prevention and amelioration of specific illnesses through improved nutrition was entirely possible. The Department of Agriculture's study attempted to find the cause, rather than just the symptom of disease. Clinicians participating in this study were convinced that if we, as individuals, learned how to take care of our own health through advances in nutritional knowledge, the economic, social, and personal implications would be enormous. The federal government was aware of the advantages of improved nutrition, but kept this information from the American people. It is impossible to place a dollar figure on the degrees of pain and loss of life that could have been avoided had the government promoted the benefits of nutrition back in 1971.

APPENDIX B

BENEFITS FROM HUMAN NUTRITION RESEARCH

True Health's President, Richard Stokley, attempted to acquire *Benefits From Human Nutrition Research* from the federal government in the late 1980s, after seeing the Canadian nutritional manufacturer, Quest's, copy of the publication. Barry Carlson, President of Quest, had received a university's copy of the study through a friend. Carlson told the author it was his understanding that an intense lobbying effort by the meat and dairy industries caused the federal government to recall *Benefits From Human Nutrition Research* shortly after its release. Over the years, Carlson made copies of the study for friends and business acquaintances. He even attempted to convince the *National Enquirer* to print excerpts of the study, but the *Enquirer* considered it "too hot to handle."

When Stokley called the Department of Agriculture and the FDA to request the study, both government agencies denied its existence. Stokley then enlisted the help of his friend, Dick Arlington, who was a member of the Conservative Political Action Committee and had connections with elected government officials. One of these officials managed to locate the nutritional study in the Department of Agriculture; Arlington was told it was "the only copy in existence." Arlington was given the book "on loan," and he, in turn, gave it to Stokley.

That the Department of Agriculture kept just one copy of a $30 million nutritional study is hard to believe, unless, of course, *Benefits From Human Research* was recalled by the federal government. The author was unsuccessful in her attempts to locate the study in Government Document departments of main libraries throughout the country. It is interesting to note, however, that the Dallas Public Library has a copy of *Human Nutrition, Report No. 1, A Survey Of Research On Human Nutrition*, which detailed the moneys spent by the federal government on human nutrition research in 1968-69. But while Report No. 1 revealed that the federal government allocated approximately $30 million to human nutrition research, it did not discuss or evaluate the *benefits* of nutrition. The Dallas Public Library has no record of *Benefits From Human Nutrition Research, Report No. 2*.

Bob Norton, spokesperson for the Department of Agriculture's Human Nutrition Center in Washington, told the author in the spring of 1993 that it is possible that *Benefits From Human Nutrition Research* was "pulled back" after its initial release; he also noted that the study was registered in the National Agriculture Library as part of their inner library loan system.

On 31 October 1994 the author requested, under the Freedom of Information Act, the following information related to *Benefits From Human Nutrition Research*: (1) Was the study available to the public, and where was it distributed? (2) Was the study recalled? If so, by whom— i.e. a government agency—and why? (3) Did the meat and dairy industries lobby the federal government to recall *Benefits From Human Nutrition Research*?

Valerie N. Herberger, Acting Coordinator for the Freedom of Information office, maintained in a 12 December 1994 letter that the Department of Agriculture had searched their records and was unable to locate any information concerning *Benefits From Human Nutrition Research*. On 21 December 1994 the author received a second letter from Ms. Herberger, this time stating that the Department of Agriculture had found a copy of the study (which she enclosed). However, Ms. Herberger did not answer any of the questions posed in the October 31st letter. On 27 December 1994 the author exercised her "right to appeal" under the Freedom of Information Act and sent a letter with the original questions to the administrator in the Agriculture Research Service (ARS) of the Department of Agriculture. Seven weeks later, the Administrator, R. D. Plowman, responded with the following answers: The "few copies of the report" that had been supplied to the ARS were "depleted" within a few months; the ARS did not know where the report was distributed or if it was recalled; the ARS did not know the cost of the study or who provided the funding.

Given that the Department of Agriculture kept no records on a $30 million nutritional study, it certainly seems, in all likelihood, that

Benefits From Human Nutrition Research was recalled by the federal government. Since the study is not available in Government Document sections of libraries, the only way to locate the book is through the National Agriculture Library. The public has not been given easy (if any) access to it.

APPENDIX C

CLINICAL STUDIES

PROSTAGLANDINS/ESSENTIAL FATTY ACIDS

Three different prostaglandins, PGE1, PGE2, and PGE3 must be kept in balance in order for the body to receive beneficial results. The major health problem in America today is that people are producing an excess of PGE2 and not enough PGE1 and PGE3. PGE1 and PGE3 are anti-inflammatory, while PGE2 causes inflammation (as in arthritis). PGE1 has been shown to halt or reverse tumor growth, whereas PGE2 enhances tumor growth in rats.

Essential fatty acids promote PGE1 and PGE3. Some of the illnesses essential fatty acids have either modified or alleviated are atopic eczema, premenstrual syndrome, high cholesterol levels, alcoholism, Sjogren's Syndrome (dry eye), hyperactivity, hypertension, diabetes, obesity, arthritis, and coronary disorders.

Gamma-Linolenic Acid (GLA)

In the 1980s, GLA was studied more intensively than any other nutrient: About 200 clinical trials took place in university hospitals and medical schools throughout the world. Dr. Horrobin's clinical studies have led him to believe that a lack of essential fatty acids could turn out to be one of the most common defects in human biochemistry and a significant factor in many diseases. Essential fatty acids are especially important in the function of nerve, muscle, and immune systems, for when people lack the proper balance, the neurological, endocrine, and immune systems are shown to be adversely affected.

GLA has proven to be effective in the treatment of many serious diseases. Double-blind, placebo-controlled studies for **atopic eczema** demonstrate that GLA improves skin conditions, relieves itching, and reduces the amount of steroid medication required. In a large, placebo-controlled trial at Bristol University in England, both adults and children showed substantial improvements. In clinical trials for **diabetes**, GLA has reversed neurological damage and lowered plasma cholesterol and triglycerides. Evening primrose oil has also been shown to be beneficial in the treatment of **Sjogren's Syndrome**. A study of untreatable patients at Glasgow University in Scotland, and a placebo-controlled trial at the University of Copenhagen, have demonstrated the effectiveness of GLA.

The English group, Action For Research of Multiple Sclerosis (ARMS), has gathered evidence that primrose oil slows down the progression of **multiple sclerosis**, and many clinical trials confirm the low amounts of essential fatty acids in the central nervous system, plasma, red blood cells, and platelets of multiple sclerosis patients.

Rheumatoid arthritis, a chronic disease affecting connective tissues of the joints, has been diminished and even stopped in some patients who use primrose oil. In this disorder of inflammation and immunity, the body is producing too many of the wrong prostaglandins (PGE2), and not enough of the right ones (PGE1). Evening primrose oil converts into PGE1, thus balancing the prostaglandins.

Women suffering from **premenstrual syndrome** are often lacking in essential fatty acids. A 1981 clinical trial at St. Thomas' Hospital in London (a major PMS clinic) studied the effect of evening primrose oil on sixty-eight severe cases of PMS. Sixty-one percent showed a marked improvement, 23 percent showed partial relief, and only 15 percent showed no change in their symptoms. Placebo-controlled trials conducted at the Universities of Dundee, Wales, Lund, and Helsinki also confirm the effectiveness of primrose oil in the treatment of PMS.

Chronic **alcohol abuse** can interfere with essential fatty acid and prostaglandin metabolism. In a double-blind, placebo-controlled study at Craig Dunain Hospital in Inverness, Scotland, Drs. Iain and Evelyn Glen observed that alcoholics undergoing withdrawal experienced fewer and less intense withdrawal symptoms when taking primrose oil. Dr. Stephen Cunnane of the Efamol Research Institute and Dr. David Segarnick, associated with the New York Veterans Administration Medical Center in New York City and the Department of Psychiatry at the New York University School of Medicine, have both found that evening primrose oil can substantially reduce liver damage caused by alcohol: The oil works to reduce the withdrawal symptoms of alcoholics, repair liver and other cellular damage caused by excessive alcohol, repair brain changes caused by alcohol, and restore certain cognitive abilities lost because of alcoholism.

The immune system is perhaps our first line of defense against **cancer.** In orthodox cancer therapy, treatment is aimed at the destruction of cancer cells with chemotherapy and radiation, and non-cancerous cells are damaged in the process. However, in test tube experiments, evening primrose oil has been shown to stimulate the T-cells of the immune system, reverting cancer cells back to normal cells. Mainstream medicine has paid very little attention to the possibility of normalizing cancer cells. Dr. Horrobin observes:

"Cancer therapy is dominated by the idea that treatment must aim at destruction of cancer cells. Since the purpose of [chemotherapy and radiation therapy] is to produce damage, it is not surprising that they harm normal cells. . . The goal is to exploit some difference between the cancer cells and the normal cells, which [will] allow the cancerous ones to be selectively destroyed."

Eicosapentanoic Acid (EPA)

EPA is found in the oils of cold-saltwater fish such as herring, haddock, cod, mackerel, sardine, and salmon, and is recognized as a powerful weapon in the fight against heart disease. EPA improves the viscosity of blood, controls spasms of the arteries and blood clotting, and lowers cholesterol and triglyceride levels.

Clinical studies show that the reason Eskimos and Japanese populations have such low rates of **heart disease, diabetes, high blood pressure, and many cancers,** is because Eskimos eat more than three-quarters of a pound of fish a day, while the Japanese average more than a quarter of a pound a day.

In 1985 the *New England Journal of Medicine* published a famous Dutch study that investigated the relationship between fish consumption and coronary disease in a group of men in the Netherlands. Dutch researchers reported on a twenty-year survey of the diets of 852 middle-aged men: Those who ate at least one ounce of fish a day had half the rate of **heart disease** of men who ate little or no fish; mortality from coronary heart disease was more than 50 percent lower among those who consumed at least 30 grams of fish per day than among those who did not eat fish.

In a clinical study of thirty-seven adults with **rheumatoid arthritis**, Dr. Joel Kremer of Albany Medical College found that those who were given a fish-oil supplement had less morning stiffness and fewer tender joints than did those who had not received the supplement. In another trial at New York's Stony Brook University, Robert Hitzemann gave fish oil to fifteen **migraine sufferers** and eight improved significantly, reporting longer intervals between attacks and fewer severe headaches. Studies at the National Institutes of Health and at Massachusetts General Hospital determined that a diet rich in Omega-3 fatty acids protected mice against **kidney disease**. And at Rutgers University in New Jersey, essential fatty acids slowed the development and progression of **mammary cancer** in rodents. The American Heart Association has advocated fish oils for those at risk of **cardiovascular disease**.

APPENDIX D

NEW DRUG APPLICATION PROCEDURE

The FDA's Office of Scientific Evaluation assigns the drug to the appropriate division, which denies, approves or suggests changes in a company's application for an Investigational New Drug. If approved, the company goes to Phase One, clinical tests on healthy people. In Phase Two, sick patients are tested (one group with placebos), and by Phase Three, "safety" is presumed and "effectiveness" becomes the criteria. The new drug is then placed in wide experimental use, and if Phase Three is successful, the company can then file for a New Drug Application. Once all the data on the drug is summarized, the drug can be marketed. Of course the process can be terminated at any time, since the FDA has veto powers in all stages of the application.

APPENDIX E

FTC COURT ORDER REQUESTING PERMANENT INJUNCTION

COMPLAINT For Permanent Injunction and Other Ancillary Relief: Defendants' Violations of Sections 5(a) and 12 of the FTC Act - "Sec. 5(a) of the FTC Act, 15 U.S.C. 45(a), makes unlawful unfair or deceptive acts or practices in or affecting commerce. Section 12(a) of the FTC Act, 15 U.S.C. 52(a) makes unlawful the dissemination of any false advertisement in or affecting commerce for the purpose of inducing, or which is likely to induce, the purchase of food, drugs, devices or cosmetics. Consumers have been injured and will continue to be injured by defendants' violations."

APPENDIX F

NINTH AMENDMENT ARGUMENTS

Stokley was prepared to defend his case in court with the following arguments, which were designed by Conrad LeBeau, lawyer and editor of the *Health Freedom Reporter*:

The right to "freedom of choice in medicine" for the buyer, seller, and manufacturer.

The right of the manufacturer to produce products for sale to the public for health purposes of both a preventive and healing nature.

The manufacturer reserves the right to use testimonials, which to the best of his knowledge and belief, are true, to promote the sale of its products.

NOTES

INNOCENT CASUALTIES contains facts and information available in government studies, scientific journals, recent books, and news reports.

The *Kellogg Report* (funded by grants from the W.K. Kellogg Foundation and the Ford Foundation) is a thorough account of the state of health in the United States today. It is referred to as *Kellogg* in the notes below.

The Department of Agriculture's 1971 study, *Benefits from Human Nutrition Research*, is referred to as *BFHNR*.

CHAPTER ONE: TRUE HEALTH

3   "A vast reservoir...human nutrition." *BFHNR*, 1.

3-4   "The American diet...nutritional supplements to maintain good health." *Kellogg*, 142-143.

3-4   "Fresh foods...vitamin content." G. Edward Griffin, *World with-out Cancer: The Story of Vitamin B17* (Westlake Village, 1980), 57; True Health research material; Morgenthaler and Fowkes, *Stop the FDA: Save Your Health Freedom*, (Menlo Park, 1992), 125.

4   "I made a decision...and do something." Author's interview with Richard Stokley, May 1992.

5   **Sources re: Prostaglandins:** "2 Swedes and Briton Win Nobel for Clues to Body's Chemistry" *New York Times*, 12 October 1982, sec. C, 3; Ann Louise Gittleman, *Beyond Pritikin* (New York, 1988); Judy Graham, *Evening Primrose Oil* (Great Britain, 1987); Jean D. Wilson, M.D. and Daniel W. Foster, M.D., *Textbook of Endocrinology* (Philadelphia, 1985).

5   **Sources re: Essential Fatty Acids:** Gittleman, *Beyond Pritikin*; Graham, *Evening Primrose Oil*; Wilson and Foster, *Textbook of Endocrinology*.

5-7   "It caught me...perked me up"; "My mother...how much my mother was helped"; "Let's get the best doctors...we were on the right track." Author's interview with Richard Stokley, May 1992.

7   "No other nutritional...its staff." True Health videotape.

8   "One of my...very impressive." True Health videotape.

9   "Dr. Tam has noticed...lower insulin requirements." True Health videotape.

9-10   "I suffered from...to improve." Author's interview with Pam Chaplin, 10 June 1992, 25 March 1995.

10   "I take *True Health*...proof of that." Author's interview with Lennie Meyers, 17 June 1992, 3 June 1995.

11   "I started taking...and so forth." Author's interview with Bill Sanders (pseudonym), 11 July 1992, 25 March 1995.

CHAPTER TWO: EVENING PRIMROSE OIL—"UNFIT FOR HUMAN CONSUMPTION"

13-14   "I was about...primrose oil"; "We were more...recovered our money." Author's interview with Richard Stokley, May 1992.

14-15   "Over 200 worldwide clinical trials...carcinogenicity studies were negative as well." Carter, "Gamma-Linolenic Acid as a Nutrient," 76; Gittleman, *Beyond Pritikin*; Graham, *Evening Primrose Oil*.

16-18   Stokley's 7 June 1988 telephone conversation with FDA Agent John Thomas. True Health's transcription of conversation.

19-20   "Scrivener had a suggestion...demands." Author's interview with Richard Stokley, Ann Stokley, and Earl Milton, May 1992.

CHAPTER THREE: TRUE HEALTH'S AIDS TEST

23-24   "Most of the world...diagnosed with AIDS." Randy Shilts, *And the Band Played On: Politics, People and the AIDS Epidemic* (New York, 1987).

25   "Someone said to me...extremely interested." Author's interview with Richard Stokley, May 1992.

25   "Dr. Pulse had attended...investigate all avenues." Terry Pulse, M.D., speaking at Center for Healing. True Health audiotape.

26-33   **True Health's clinical trial:** T.L. Pulse, M.D., and Elizabeth Uhlig, "A Significant Improvement in a Clinical Pilot Study Utilizing Nutritional Supplements, Essential Fatty Acids and Stabilized Aloe Vera Juice in 29 Seropositive, ARC and AIDS Patients," *J of Advancement in Medicine* (1990): 209-230.

26   "I want my research...study would include." True Health videotape.

27   "As the study...synergism of all three." True Health videotape.

28   "We did not ...he was doing." Author's interview with Richard Stokley, May 1992.

28-29   "We came to Dallas...of the illness." True Health videotape.

29   "I think the...health back again." True Health videotape.

29-30   "It looks like...tells the story." Author's interview with Richard Stokley, May 1992.

30-32   AIDS test patients "E", "S," and "D" testimonies. True Health videotape.

32   "Dr. U.N. Das hypothesized...fatty acids." "Can Essential Fatty Acid Deficiency Predispose to AIDS?" *Can Med Assoc J* 132 (1985): 900.

32   "Malnutrition is common...people with AIDS." C. Huang, et al. "Nutritional Status of Patients with AIDS," *Clinical Chemistry* 34 no. 10 (1988): 1957-1959.

33   "If we don't do something...nothing to lose." True Health videotape.

CHAPTER FOUR: THE MEDIA—AN INSTRUMENT FOR GOVERNMENT PROPAGANDA

35   "We were not...to the press." Author's interview with Richard Stokley, May 1992.

36   "After True Health...under our jurisdiction." "Officials Scrutinizing AIDS Nutrition Pack," *Dallas Morning News*, July 1989.

37   "Jacobson quoted FDA media spokesman...patients at the news conference." Ibid.

37   "We had Walter Reed...seropositive." True Health videotape of news conference.

37-38   "Jacobson further disparaged...challenged his personal and professional ethics." "Controversy Plagues AIDS Doctor's Career," *Dallas Morning News*, 6 September 1989, 1, 10a, 11a.

38   "The only other newspaper...by the media." "Diet Supplement for AIDS Patients Touted, Questioned," *Wichita Falls Times Record*, 6 September 1989, sec. A, 1.

38   "An advertising executive...money from the pharmaceutical industry." Author's interview with Pierce Beneke, June 1992.

CHAPTER FIVE: INNOCENT CASUALTIES IN A WAR

41-43   FDA agents Martinez and Davis at True Health offices. True Health written record of meeting, 2 August 1989.

43   "A few days later, Joel Martinez...innocent casualties." Author's interview with Richard Stokley, May 1992, and Elizabeth Uhlig, November 1994.

43   **180-Day AIDS Test Results:** Pulse, "A Significant Improvement ...AIDS Patients," 209-230; Phyllis Rueckert, Ph.D,*Statistical Analysis of AIDS Research Data—180 Day Report*, (Center for Statistical Consulting and Research: Southern Methodist University, November 1989).

43   "Dr. Donald B. Owen...immune systems had been restarted." Author's interview with Richard Stokley, May 1992.

44   "Harold Davis at the FDA...True Health's formula." Author's interview with Richard Stokley, May 1992.

CHAPTER SIX: FTC VS. INTERNATIONAL WHITE CROSS

49   "Charging that Immune Plus...treatments to forego them." "FTC Charges Producers and Marketers of 'Immune Plus' with Making False Claims about Its Ability to Cure AIDS," *FTC News*, 7 February 1991, 1.

49-52   Court testimonies taken from Government Documents. Federal Trade Commission v. International White Cross, Inc., et al., U.S. District Court, Northern District of California, 1991.

49-51   FDA agents Zeigler and Brinck at True Health offices. True Health videotape, 20 December 1990.

53   **Stipulated Final Judgement and Order for Permanent Injunction:** Federal Trade Commission v. International White Cross, Inc, et al.; C-91-0377-TEH, 22 October 1991.

53   FDA agents threatened to seize UPS records. Author's interview with Richard Stokely, May 1992, and Elizabeth Uhlig, November 1994.

54   "Attorney Jay Geller...issues." The Burton Goldberg Group, *Alternative Medicine: The Definitive Guide*, 19.

54   "Marion Moss...providers and minor companies." "Why Isn't the FDA Doing Its Job?" *Alternative Medicine Digest* no. 1, 3.

54   "AIDS patients are calling...need it have it." True Health documents.

CHAPTER SEVEN: THE FDA—AS DANGEROUS AS THE WORST
DISEASE

65   "The thing that bugs...night and day." Griffin, *World without
      Cancer*, 395.

65   "Unrelenting in its war...dangers of prescription drugs."
      "Alternative Medicine Backers Plan Rally," *Dallas Morning
      News*, 10 August 1992, sec. A, 3; "Revoke FDA Authority over
      the Nutritional Marketplace," *Health Store News*, (April/May
      1992): 1; Griffin, *World without Cancer*; *Dietary Supplement Health
      and Education Act of 1994* (October 1994), 14-17.

66   "The Pure Food and Drug Act...stringent regulation of vitamins
      and minerals." Steven Friedman and Robert E. Burger, *Forbidden
      Cures* (New York, 1976), 11-15; Morton Mintz, *By Prescription
      Only* (Boston, 1967), 248-264; Milton Silverman and Philip R.
      Lee, *Pills, Profits and Politics* (San Francisco, 1974), 94-96; The
      Burton Goldberg Group, *Alternative Medicine: The Definitive
      Guide* (Puyallup, 1994), 18-19.

66   Thalidomide as an AIDS treatment. "Banned in the U.S. for
      Causing Birth Defects, Thalidomide Returns as an AIDS
      Drug,"*Wall Street Journal*, 25 June 1995, sec. B, 1.

66-67 "In 1962, the FDA...combination, and potency desired." *Dietary
      Supplement Health and Education Act of 1994*, 14-17.

67   "In the fall of 1971...and the AMA." Robert C. Atkins, *Dr. Atkins'
      Health Revolution* (Boston, 1988), 10-13; Griffin, *World without
      Cancer*, 404.

67   "In 1985, the Pharmaceutical Advertising Council...with the
      antiquackery campaign." The Burton Goldberg Group,
      Alternative Medicine: The Definitive Guide, 20.

67-68 "The orthodox medical establishment...their licenses revoked."
      "The Scoop on Vitamins," *Time* (6 April 1992): 54-56; Atkins,
      Health Revolution, 13; "Cold War over Vitamin C Rages On,"
      Boston Globe, 28 December 1992, 36.

68   "For years, the AMA engaged...7th Circuit on 7 February 1990."
      The Burton Goldberg Group, *Alternative Medicine: The Definitive
      Guide*, 20.

68   "Despite the passage...natural food substances." *Dietary Supplement Health and Education Act of 1994*, 14-17.

68-69   "In the early 1990s...won't be on the shelves." "Agents Raiding Health Food Stores," *Fort Worth Star-Telegram*, 9 August 1992, 4; "Alternative Medicine Backers Plan Rally," *Dallas Morning News*, 10 August 1992, sec. A, 3; "Legislate, Litigate, Indoctrinate and Intimidate," *Health Store News* (April/May 1992): 4-5; "Seizures of Health Food Stir Outcry," *Dallas Morning News*, 6 July 1992, sec. B, 11; "Texas Health Officials Hit Ye Seekers,"*Health Foods Business* (July 1992): 12, 22; "The New Scoop on Vitamins," *Time* (6 April 1992): 59.

69   "In its May 1992...for drug development." *FDA Dietary Supplements Task Force Final Report—June 1992.*

69-70   "On March 31, 1993...approved drug applications." *Alternative Medicine Digest* no. 1, 3.

70   "In 1993...in seven states." "Just Call Me 'Doc'," *Forbes* (22 November 1992): 108-110.

71   "Orthodox medicine...accept the truth." Atkins, *Health Revolution*, 4-13.

71   "Doctors are not consciously...in between." Griffin, *World without Cancer*, 369-382.

71   "In 1984, the Committee...medical profession." *Kellogg*, 562.

72   "Patents used to...protection period." "FDA Ruling Will Extend Brand-Name Drug Patents," *Los Angeles Times*, 8 June 1995, sec. D, 5.

72   "During the 1980s...their biggest expense." "Huge Profits of Pharmaceutical Companies," *Prime Time Live*, 18 June 1992; "Taking Aim At High Drug Prices," *Boston Globe*, 28 February 1993, 73.

72   "Pharmaceutical ad campaigns...at their word." *Kellogg*, 209, 301; Bruce Nussbaum, *Good Intentions* (New York, 1987), 32; "Not What the Doctor Ordered," *Newsweek* (8 June 1992): 54.

73   "A revolving door...they had regulated." *Alternative Digest* no. 1, 3.

73   "In 1975, the General Accounting...Exchange Commission."
        Alternative Digest no. 1, 3; Morgenthaler and Fowkes, *Stop the
        FDA: Save Your Health Freedom* (Menlo Park), 138.

73-74   Drugs Versus Nutrients: "Drugs are foreign to the body...toxic
        side effects." *Kellogg*, 84.

74   "At least 130,000 Americans...drug reactions." "FDA
        Misbranded Drugs; Kills, Injures Millions," *Health Freedom
        Report*, (July/August/September 1991): 1, 4.

74   "The only cases...megadoses for months on end." "Vitamins,"
        Time (6 April 1992): 59; "Please Kill or Amend HR 1662," *Health
        Store News* (April/May 1992): 20.

77   Halcion. "FDA Advisors Say Halcion Is Safe, Suggest New
        Label," *Dallas Morning News*, 19 May 1992, sec. A, 1, 8; "Fueling
        the Fire over Halcion: Upjohn's Own Staff Has Raised Safety
        Concerns," *Newsweek* (25 May 1992): 84; "Halcion: A Damaging
        Report," *Newsweek* (2 May 1994): 6.

78   "FDA regularly approves...tested by the FDA." Griffin, *World
        without Cancer*, 402-403; *Kellogg*, 184.

78   "One in three...experience cancer." "Cancer Facts & Figures—
        1992," American Cancer Society brochure.

78   "There is growing evidence...had been documented." *Kellogg*,
        184.

78   "Recent studies demonstrate...contracting childhood leukemia."
        "The Hazards of Eating Hot Dogs," *Delicious Magazine*
        (September 1994): 14.

78-79   "As current regulations...poses any health risk"; "According
        to...yet to follow suit." "A Mystery in Your Lunchbox,"
        Newsweek (8 June 1992): 48-51; "A Needless Risk of Breast
        Cancer," editorial by Samuel S. Epstein: *Los Angeles Times*, 20
        March 1994, sec. M, 5; "Bitter Medicine for the Drug
        Companies," *U.S. News & World Report* (24 October 1994): 72;
        "First Genetically Altered Food Approved by FDA," *Los Angeles
        Times*, 19 May, 1994, sec. A, 1, 28; "Fried Gene Tomatoes," *Time*
        (30 May 1994): 54; "Genetically Engineered Food is Ripe—But
        Are We Ready?" *Delicious Magazine* (September 1994): 11-12;
        "Health Watch—Who Uses rBGH?" *Let's Live* (May 1995): 8.

CHAPTER EIGHT: AN UNDERCOVER DICTATORSHIP

81   "FDA continues to deny...applications of nutritional supplements." Morgenthaler and Fowkes, *Stop the FDA*, 28.

82   "David Kessler became...office during the day." "Just Call Me Doc," *Forbes* (22 November 1993): 110.

82   "FDA attempted to circumvent...never at issue." *Dietary Supplement Health and Education Act of 1994* (October 1994), 16.

82-83   **Traco Labs Court Case:** "FDA Case Against BCO Is Dismissed," *Health Foods Business* (July 1992): 12; "FDA, You Are in Wonderland (So Rule the Courts)," *Let's Live* (March 1993): 14; "Setting the FDA Straight," *Health Foods Business* (June 1991): 6; *Dietary Supplement Health and Education Act of 1994* (October 1994), 16.

83-84   **CoEnzyme Q10:** "Heartless Behavior," *Texas Monthly* (June 1992): 48-55; *FDA Dietary Supplements Task Force Final Report— June 1992*, 16.

84-86   **FDA raid of Dr. Jonathan Wright's Office:** "Answers Needed on Vitamin Raid," *Journal American*, 13 May 1992, sec. A, 8; "Armed Agents Make 'B-Vitamin Bust' in Kent," *Seattle Post Intelligencer*, 7 May 1992, sec. A, 1; "FDA's Strange Raid," *Seattle Post Intelligencer*, 11 May 1992, sec. A, 9; "Workers at Raided Kent Clinic Contradict Police Reports," *The Morning News Tribune*, 15 May 1992, sec. B, 3; "FDA Raids Respected Natural Doctor," *Let's Live* (June 1992): 10; "For Immediate Release," *Citizens for Health Report on Jonathan Wright Raid*; Dr. Wright speaking at American College for the Advancement of Medicine meeting, Dallas, 15 May 1992. "FDA Commissioner...themselves." *Let the Truth Be the Bias: How the FDA Maneuvers Politically to Cast Stigma on Alternative M.D.s.* videotape; The Burton Goldberg Group, *Alternative Medicine: The Definitive Guide*, 23-25.

86-88   **L-Tryptophan Ban:** "An Industry Unmonitored," *Newsweek* (7 June 1993): 52; "FDA Acts to Control Vitamin Claims," *New York Times*, 9 August, 1992, sec. A, 1; "Industry Voices Opposition to Amino Acid Initiative," *Health Food Business* (July 1992): 16; "Legislate, Litigate, Indoctrinate and Intimidate," *Health Store News* (April/May 1992): 4-5; Morgenthaler and Fowkes, *Stop the*

FDA, 126, 132, 150; "The FDA's Newspeak," *Let's Live* (September 1992): 1, 75; The Burton Goldberg Group, *Alternative Medicine: The Definitive Guide*, 24.

88-90   **NLEA Act and FDA Asks For Police-State Powers:** "A Good Concept Gone Bad," *Health Store News* (April/May 1992): 1-2; "An Industry Unmonitored," *Newsweek* (7 June 1993): 52-53; "Consumer Protection or Freedom from Choice," *Vegetarian Times* (May 1992): 4; *Dietary Supplement Health and Education Act of 1994* (October 1994): 15-16; "NNFA Grapevine," *Let's Live* (September 1992): 14; "One Million Jobs Affected by FDA Regulations," *Health Store News* (April/May 1992): 1, 23; "Take Action!" *Delicious* (May/June 1992): 8; "The FDA's Newspeak," *Let's Live,* (September 1992): 1, 75; "Understanding the Congressional and FDA Bills and Regulations," *Health Store News* (April/May 1992): 3; "Restarting the Engine of Change," *Health Food Business* (July 1992): 6; "FDA's Legal Moves to Limit Dietary Supplementation," *Health Store News* (April/May 1992): 19; "The NLEA May Be the Demise of the Proxmire Amendment," *Health Store News* (April/May 1992): 16; "Please Kill or Amend HR 1662," *Health Store News* (April/May 1992): 20.

90   "1992 Task Force...in near future." "The FDA's Newspeak," *Let's Live* (September 1992): 1, 75.

90-91   "Both the *Los Angeles Times*...was dietary supplements." "Save My Emulsified Rhino Tusks," *Los Angeles Times*, 27 December 1993, sec. A, 5; "The Snake Oil Protection Act," 5 October 1993, sec. A, 1.

91   "Influenced more by...in a Senate hearing." "FDA Enforcement Bill Draws Widespread Opposition," *Health Foods Business* (July 1992): 18.

91-92   **Hatch Legislation:** "Down the Hatch—Utah Senator Plugs Health Freedom Act to Counter Waxman Bill," *Los Angeles Reader*, 14 August 1992, 12; "FDA Enforcement Bill Draws Widespread Opposition," *Health Foods Business* (July 1992): 18; "FDA's Current Position On Herbs," *New England Health Freedom Awareness Week* brochure; "Health Freedom vs. the FDA: The Final Fight Begins," *Let's Live* (June 1993): 48; *Dietary Supplement Health and Education Act of 1994* (October 1994), 16-17.

92   "Kessler adamantly argued...about their products." "Senate Panel Votes to Delay Vitamin Rules," *Los Angeles Times*, 12 May 1994, sec. A, 14.

92   "The public can be assured...not be altered." "FDA Says It Won't Restrict Dietary Supplements," *Los Angeles Times*, 15 December 1993, sec. A, 5.

92   "FDA had very little data...testing." "Congress Fails to Halt Curbs on Vitamin Labels," *Los Angeles Times*, 27 November 1993, sec. A, 24.

92-93   **Dietary Supplement Health and Education Act of 1994:** "House OKs Bill on Vitamin Benefit Claims." *Los Angeles Times*, 8 October 1994, sec. A, 16; *Dietary Supplement Health and Education Act of 1994* (October 1994).

93   Less than two months...files and ledgers." *Citizens For Health Report*, 3 no. 1 (1995): 1, 7.

94   ***Publishers Weekly* Article**: "An Alternative View of Alternative Medicine: The Government's," *Publishers Weekly* (19 September 1994): 42.

CHAPTER NINE: ACQUIRED IMMUNE DEFICIENCY SYNDROME

96   "Smallpox Vaccine...incidence of AIDS in South America." "Smallpox Vaccine 'Triggered AIDS Virus'," *London Times*, 11 May 1987, 1, 18.

96   "Contaminated polio vaccines...polio-like diseases." Douglass, "Who Murdered Africa," *Health Freedom News*, 42; *The Strecker Memorandum*; "Origins of a Plague," *U.S. News & World Report* (30 March 1992) 50-52.

96   "An attempt should...responding to the virus." World Health Organization—1972, *Bulletin*, 47: 251.

96-97   **House of Commons Report:** United Kingdom, *Problems Associated with AIDS*, Commons, vol. III, Session 1986, (1987).

97   "Robert B. Strecker...radio advertising time." *The Strecker Memorandum*, videotape.

97   *London Times* has been openly critical...and WHO estimate." "A Word War over AIDS," *Prodigy*, 20 December 1993.

97   **African green monkey transferred AIDS to man:** Douglass, "Who Murdered Africa," *Health Freedom News*, 19; "The Future of AIDS," *Newsweek* (22 March 1993): 47-52; "Origins of a Plague," *U.S. News & World Report* (30 March 1992): 50-52.

97   **Green monkey theory ludicrous:** "Is the HIV AIDS Theory All Wrong?" *Faculty*, Cal Report/Fall 1991.

98   "The Social Services Committee...the conventional wisdom." United Kingdom, *Problems Associated with AIDS*, Commons, 1986-1987.

98   "American homosexuals...hepatitis vaccine studies." Douglass, "Who Murdered Africa," *Health Freedom News*, 42; *The Strecker Memorandum*.

98   "Surgeon General's...from a kiss." U.S. Department of Health & Human Services, *Understanding AIDS* (1988).

99   **Harvard's AIDS Projection:** "Harvard AIDS Study Sees 120 Million Infections by Decade's End," *Boston Globe*, 4 June 1992, 15.

99   "Between 1986...will be lost due to AIDS." "The Hidden Cost of AIDS," *U.S. News & World Report* (27 July 1992): 49-59.

99-100 **Dr. Duesberg's Theory:** "Is the HIV AIDS Theory All Wrong?" *Faculty*, Cal Report/Fall 1991; Jon Rappoport, *AIDS Inc.— Scandal of the Century* (Foster City), 113.

100   "Robert Root-Bernstein, Ph.D....AIDS in anyone." Leon Chaitow, N.D., D.O. and Strohecker, *You Don't Have to Die: Unraveling the AIDS Myth* (Washington), 9.

100   "Duesberg charges that...$3 billion on HIV research." "Is the HIV AIDS Theory All Wrong?" *Faculty*, Cal Report/Fall 1991.

101   "Scientists researching... for Gallo." Rappoport, *AIDS Inc.*, 87.

101   "If there are still...a year after its discovery!" "Is the HIV AIDS Theory All Wrong?" *Faculty*, Cal Report/ Fall 1991.

101-102 "It's a selection process...high-stakes science, financially." Rappoport, *AIDS Inc.*, 125, 141, 143.

102   "Gary Bauer...that can be proved." Ibid, 94.

102-103 **Who Discovered HIV:** "American Scientist Who Found HIV Is Investigated Anew," *New York Times*, 2 March 1992, sec. A, 1, 10; Shilts, *And the Band Played On*, 1987.

103-104 **The "New AIDS Virus":** "CDC's Image Tarnished by Its Handling of AIDS Issues," *Dallas Morning News*, 2 August 1992, sec. J, 1; "AIDS-Like Illness Debated," *Dallas Morning News*, 24 July 1992, sec. A, 17; "Scientists Look Beyond HIV for the Causes of AIDS," *Los Angeles Daily News*, 11 May 1992, 7; Chaitow and Strohecker, *You Don't Have to Die*, 9; "International Classification of Diseases, 10th Edition," *World Health Organization* (Geneva, 1992).

104-105 "Only 68 cases...Japanese scientists reported...recipients of his blood are perfectly healthy." "AIDS—Words from the Front," *Spin* (March 1993): 53, 75.

105   "*The Lancet* reported...the original diagnosis." G. Duffort, et al.: "No Clinical Signs Fourteen Years after HIV-2 Transmission Via Blood Transfusion," *The Lancet*, 2 no. 8069 (27 September 1988): 510.

105   "Michael Lange, M.D....other factors may be." J. Learment, et al.: "Long-Term Symptomless HIV-1 Infection in Recipients of Blood Products from a Single Donor," *The Lancet*, 340 no. 8824 (3 October 1992): 863-7.

105   "Medical data suggests...still free of AIDS." Chaitow and Strohecker, *You Don't Have to Die*, 30, 32.

105   "Whether condoms can...penetration of HIV." Ibid., 43.

106   "A growing number...AIDS on its own." Ibid., 45.

106   **AIDS Statistics Artificially Inflated:** "AIDS: Experts Pessimistic," *Los Angeles Times*, 8 August 1994, sec. A, 11; "AIDS Is No. 1 Killer of Young Americans," *Los Angeles Times*, 2 December 1994, sec. A, 8; A.J. France, "Changing Case-Definition for AIDS," *The Lancet*, 340 no. 8832 (5 December

1992): 1414; "Seeking a Cure: Faith, Frustration," *Los Angeles Times*, 7 August 1994, sec. A, 1, 18-19; CRS Report for Congress—July 15, 1993. Mortality Data taken from U.S. Department of Health & Human Services, Centers for Disease Control & Prevention, National Health Statistics. Advance Report of Final Report of Final Mortality Statistics, 1990, *Monthly Vital Statistics Report*, 41, no. 7, Supplement, (7 January 1993).

CHAPTER TEN: POLITICAL AGENDAS

107   Duesberg quote, "There has never...companies grow." Rappoport, *AIDS, Inc.*, 115.

107   "Those who are...suppresses it." Ibid., 163.

108   **Magic Johnson announced his retirement:** "Magic," *Sports Illustrated* (18 November 1991); "A Magical Career Comes to an End," *The Sporting News*, 18 November 1991, 9-15; *Los Angeles Times* articles, November 1991.

108-109 "Since 1983, desperate AIDS victims...had been circumventing...." "In AZT's First Year of Sales, Burroughs Wellcome Made $200 Million in Profits," Nussbaum, *Good Intentions*.

109-110 "From 1982 until...and the placebo group." Chaitow and Strohecker, *You Don't Have to Die*, 20.

109   "Number of potential AZT users...a million." "For Users of AZT, Some Sobering News," *Newsweek* (24 February 1992): 63.

110   **February 1992 AZT study:** Neil Graham, et al., "The Effects on Survival of Early Treatment of Human Immunodeficiency Virus Infection," *NE J Med* (1992): 1037-1042.

110   **Concorde Study:** "Concorde: MRC/ANRS Randomized Double-Blind Controlled Trial of Immediate and Deferred Zidovudine in Symptom-free HIV Infection," *The Lancet*, 343 (8 April 1994): 871-880.

110   "As a chemotherapy drug...introgenic genocide." "The Dark Side of the FDA," *Whole Life Times*, (October 1992): 19.

110   **Costs of AZT:** Nussbaum, *Good Intentions*.

110   "AZT has not saved...adhere to the 'AIDS Establishment'."
Rappoport, *AIDS, Inc.*, 202.

110-111 "In an effort to...die if they don't take AZT." "County Weighs
HIV Tests of Pregnant Women," *Los Angeles Times*, 20 December
1994; "Locking HIV Out of the Womb," *Newsweek* (7 March
1994): 53; "Whose Life Is It?" *Los Angeles Times*, 7 February 1995,
sec. E, 1-5.

111   "After over a decade...destroy healthy cells." *AIDS, Inc.*, 22;
"FDA Approves Fourth Drug for Treatment of AIDS, HIV," *Los
Angeles Times*, 28 June 1994, sec. A, 4.

111   "In the spring of 1995...of the disease." "New Drugs Offer Hope
in Battle Against AIDS," *Los Angeles Times*, 1 February 1995, sec.
A, 1, 13.

111   **10th International AIDS Conference:** "AIDS: Experts
Pessimistic," *Los Angeles Times*, 8 August 1994, Sec. A, 11; "Battle
Fatigue: Scant Hope Emerges from This Year's AIDS Meeting,"
Time (22 August 1994): 63.

EPILOGUE

113-115 "I feel it of greatest...first step to recovery." Author's interview
with Randy Koppang, July 1992.

116-119 "The product *True Health*...change their lifestyles." Author's
interview with Harvey Brennan (pseudonym), August 1992,
November 1994.

119   "Americans are increasingly opting for...alternative medicine
exclusively." "Health Fraud Campaign Is the Real Health
Fraud," *Alive* (January/February 1992): 5.

119   "In January 1993...by the AMA." "Unconventional Cures,"
Boston Globe, 28 January 1993, 1, 11; "Local Healers," *Boston
Globe*, 26 February 1993, 25, 34; "Looking For the Cure-All,"
Boston Globe Magazine, 28 March 1993, 9-10.

119   "Due to increased public pressure...study of alternative treat-
ments." "Alternative Medicine," *Let's Live* (September 1994): 13;
"U.S. Opens the Door Just a Crack to Alternative Forms of
Medicine," *New York Times*, 10 January 1993, 1, 22.

119   "An ex-NIH employee...there's nothing there." "An Interview with Tom Harkin," *Let's Live* (September 1994): 78.

119   "According to a *Boston Globe*...narrow margin." "Funds Flowing to Guide Health Reform's Course," *Boston Globe*, 14 February 1993, 1, 24; "Health Industry Enlists Prominent Lobbyists," *Wall Street Journal*, 18 March 1993, sec. A, 14.

119-120 "Congressman Henry Waxman...insurance companies." Morgenthaler and Fowkes, *Stop the FDA*, 89.

APPENDIX A—THE BENEFITS OF NUTRITION

121   "Better health...and human nutrition topics." *BFHNR*, vii, 1.

121   "Thirty million...research project." Department of Agriculture, *Human Nutrition: Report No. 1—A Survey of Research on Human Nutrition Supported and/or Conducted by Public Research Organizations* (August 1971), iii.

122-124 "Medical costs have soared...without coverage entirely." Office of the Actuary from the Health Care Financing Administration; "Condition: Critical," *Time* (25 November 1991): 35; National Center For Health Statistics, *Healthy People 2000: National Health Promotion and Disease Prevention Objectives* (Maryland 1991).

124   "A 1992 University of Arkansas...year 2022." "Millions over 65 at Risk of Malnutrition," *Dallas Morning News*, 26 July 1992, sec. A, 1, 24.

124   "Drugs are regularly...are warranted." *Kellogg*, 315.

124   "In 1992, only three...on disease prevention." "Disease Prevention Neglected, Center Says," *Dallas Morning News*, 24 July 1992, sec. A, 7.

124   "Doctors are trained to perform bypass...chemotherapy and radiation." *Kellogg*, 315; *Alternative Medicine Digest* no. 1, 8.

124   "The American Cancer Society...potential toxicity." American Cancer Society, *Nutrition, Common Sense and Cancer*, (1984).

124   "Toxicity symptoms...perspiration." Linus C. Pauling, *Vitamin C*

and the Common Cold (New York, 1971), 63-64; John D. Kirschmann, *Nutrition Almanac* (Boston, 1979), 44.

124   "In a 1993 article...abandon effective treatment." *Alternative Medicine Digest* no. 1, 12.

124-125 "The cancer establishment...expense of prevention." "Inside the Cancer Establishment," *Ms.* (May/June 1993): 57.

125   "Despite the billions...in 30 years." *Kellogg*, 5.

125   "Since the 'war on cancer'...spending since 1971." "U.S. Panel Urges Full Overhaul of Cancer Research," *Los Angeles Times*, 30 September 1994, sec. A, 1, 15.

125   "The cancer establishment confuses the public...does it all go?" Morgenthaler and Fowkes, *Stop the FDA*, 17; "The Environmental Link to Breast Cancer," *Ms.* (May/June 1993): 56.

125   "Breast cancer is four...detection and treatment rather than prevention." "Breast Cancer Prevention: Diet vs. Drugs," *Ms.* (May/June 1993): 38-46.

125-126 "In 1969...of the American people." *Kellogg*, 115.

126   "Orthodox medicine...and fortified items." *Kellogg*, 99.

126   "Recent studies on folic...hours after birth." "Vitamins," *Newsweek* (7 June 1993): 47-48.

126-127 "A lack of antioxidants...cardiovascular disease." "How the Sick Get Sicker, Quicker, without Nutritional Supplements," *Let's Live* (January 1994): 44; "Stay Healthy," *Let's Live*, (January 1994): 8.

127   "A search of Medlars' Data Base...dietary supplements." The Burton Goldberg Group, *Alternative Medicine: The Definitive Guide*, 22.

127   **Finnish Study:** "Are You Aware? Finnish Study Is Revisited," *Let's Live*, (November 1994): 12; "Vitamin Supplements Are Seen as No Guard Against Diseases," *New York Times*, 14 April 1994, sec. A, 1, 9.

128   "In 1970, health care in the U.S...comparable economic development." *BFHNR*, 1.

128   "In 1993, health...industrialized countries." Office of the Actuary from the Health Care Financing Administration.

128   "The alleviation of nutrition-related...improving most of all."*BFHNR*, 1.

128   "Diet was believed...change in diet at a young age." *BFHNR*, 1-2.

128   "Even the small advances...development of a disease state." *BFHNR*, 1-3.

128   "Regional differences...low income families." *BFHNR*, 2.

128-129 "Directly attributable...succeeding generations." *BFHNR*, 2-3.

130-131 Chart: "...Potential Savings From Improved Diet." *BFHNR*, 4-10.

131   "Researchers determined...personal implications would be enormous." *BFHNR*, 1-3.

APPENDIX C—CLINICAL STUDIES

137-140 **Sources re: Prostaglandins:** "2 Swedes and Briton Win Nobel for Clues to Body's Chemistry," *New York Times*, 12 October 1982, sec. C, 3; Gittleman, *Beyond Pritikin*; Graham, *Evening Primrose Oil*; Wilson and Foster, *Textbook of Endocrinology*.

137-140 **Sources re: Essential Fatty Acids:** Gittleman, *Beyond Pritikin*; Graham, *Evening Primrose Oil*; Wilson and Foster, *Textbook of Endocrinology*.

137-138 "Dr. Horrobin's clinical studies...significant in many diseases." David F. Horrobin, "Gamma-Linolenic Acid in Medicine," *1984-1985 Yearbook of Nutritional Medicine*, (1985), 23-35.

138   **Atopic Eczema clinical trial:** Horrobin, "Gamma-Linolenic Acid in Medicine," 30.

138   **Diabetes clinical trials:** James P. Carter, M.D., "Gamma-Linolenic Acid as a Nutrient," *Food Technology* (1988): 74-82.

138   **Sjogren's Syndrome clinical trial:** Horrobin, "Gamma-Linolenic Acid in Medicine," 32.

138   **Action for Research of Multiple Sclerosis:** Graham, *Evening Primrose Oil*, 71-79.

138   **Rheumatoid Arthritis:** Ibid., 66-70.

138   **St. Thomas clinical trial:** Ibid., 37.

138   **Dundee, Wales, Lund, and Helsinki clinical trials:** David F. Horrobin, "Placebo-controlled Trials of Evening Primrose Oil," *Swed J Biol Med* (1984): 15.

138-139 **Craig Dunain Hospital clinical trial:** Alan Donald, "Alcoholism: The Role of Essential Fatty Acids," *Bestways* (May 1987): 22-25.

138-139 "Dr. Stephen Cunnane...because of alcoholism." Alan Donald, "Alcoholism: The Role of Essential Fatty Acids," *Bestways* (May 1987): 22-25.

139   "Mainstream...selectively destroyed." Richard S. Bockman, M.D., "Prostaglandins in Cancer: A Review," *Clin Sci Rev* (1983): 485-493; David F. Horrobin and Mehar S. Manku, "Essential Fatty Acids in Clinical Medicine," *Nutrition and Health* (1983): 127-134; Horrobin, "Gamma-Linolenic Acid in Medicine," 23-25; David F. Horrobin, et al., "The Effects of Hydrogenated Coconut Oil and Evening Primrose Oil on Development of Hypertension and Sodium Handling in Spontaneously Hypertensive Rats," *Can J Physio Pharm*, 325-330; Rashida A. Karmali, et al, "Effects of Dietary Enrichment with Gamma-Linolenic Acid Upon Growth of the R3230AC Mammary Adenocarcinoma," *J of Nutrition, Growth and Cancer* (1985): 41-51.

139-140 **Sources re: Eicosapentanoic Acid:** Gittleman, *Beyond Pritikin*; Graham, *Evening Primrose Oil*; Dianne Hales, "How Fish Can Save Your Life," *Parade Magazine* (November 1986): 17.

139   **Dutch Study:** Kromhout Daan, et al., "The Inverse Relation between Fish Consumption and 20-Year Mortality from Coronary Heart Disease," *NE J Med* (1985): 1205-1209.

140   "In a clinical study...cardiovascular disease." Hales, "How Fish Can Save Your Life," 17.

GLOSSARY

ACS: American Cancer Society

AMA: American Medical Association

AZT: (Retrovir) —The most commonly prescribed drug for people in various stages of HIV and AIDS; recommended by the CDC as they claim it delays the course of the HIV virus.

CDC: Centers For Disease Control, Atlanta

ddC/ddI: Next to AZT, the most widely prescribed drugs to combat HIV and AIDS; recommended by the CDC.

Eicosapentanoic Acid (EPA): One of the two main types of essential fatty acids; also referred to as **Omega-3**; oil obtained from fish and marine life.

Essential Fatty Acids (EFA): Unsaturated fatty acids; essential in the formation of prostaglandins; cannot be manufactured by the body.

Evening Primrose Oil: An essential fatty acid containing gamma linolenic acid; used worldwide for a variety of illnesses.

Gamma–Linolenic Acid (GLA): One of the two main types of essential fatty acids; also referred to as **Omega-6**; derived from plant and botanical sources such as evening primrose oil and unrefined vegetable oils.

GRAS (Generally Regarded As Safe): FDA label for foods regarded as safe.

HIV (Human Immunodeficiency Virus): A retrovirus; believed by the CDC to cause AIDS.

IND: Investigational New Drug

Linolenic Acid: A form of GLA

NCI: National Cancer Institute

NIAID: National Institutes of Allergies and Infectious Diseases

NIH: National Institutes of Health

OAM: Office of Alternative Medicine

PAC: Political Action Committee

Prostaglandins: Minute, hormone-like substances implicated in a wide range of human and animal illnesses; prostaglandins control all body functions at the cellular level. Essential fatty acids promote the health and growth of prostaglandins.

Retrovirus: A class of viruses which copy genetic material; HIV is considered by the CDC to be a retrovirus.

T Cells (T-lymphocytes): White blood cells that participate in a variety of cell-mediated immune reactions. There are three different types of T cells: **T4 cells** —"helper cells" that target the invading organism; **T8 cells** —"suppressor cells" that halt immune responses; **NK cells** —"natural killer cells" that attack and destroy infected body cells.

WHO: World Health Organization

BIBLIOGRAPHY

Richard Stokley provided all files, documents, videotapes, and audiotapes pertaining to True Health, Inc.

BOOKS

Atkins, Robert C. *Dr. Atkins' Health Revolution*. Boston: Houghton Mifflin Company, 1988.

Beasley, Joseph D., M.D., and Jerry J. Swift, M.A. *The Kellogg Report: The Impact of Nutrition, Environment & Lifestyle on the Health of Americans*. New York: Bard College—The Institute of Health Policy & Practice, 1989.

Chaitow, Leon, N.D., D.O., and James Strohecker. *AIDS: You Don't Have to Die—Unraveling the AIDS Myth*. Puyallup, Washington: Future Medicine Publishing, Inc., 1994.

Day, Lorraine, M.D. *AIDS: What the Government Isn't Telling You*. Palm Desert: Rockford Press, 1991.

Epstein, Samuel S., M.D. *The Politics of Cancer*. San Francisco: Sierra Club Books, 1978.

Friedman, Steven, and Robert E. Burger. *Forbidden Cures*. New York: Stein and Day Publishers, 1976.

Gittleman, Ann Louise. *Beyond Pritikin.* New York: Bantam Books, 1988.

Graham, Judy. *Evening Primrose Oil.* Great Britain: Whitstable Litho Ltd., 1987.

Griffin, G. Edward. *World without Cancer: The Story of Vitamin B_{17}.* Westlake Village: American Media, 1980.

Johnson, Earvin "Magic". *What You Can Do to Avoid AIDS.* New York: Times Books, 1992.

Kirschmann, John D. *Nutrition Almanac.* New York: McGraw-Hill Book Company, 1979.

Mintz, Morton. *By Prescription Only.* Boston: Houghton Mifflin Company, 1967.

Morgenthaler, John and Steven Wm. Fowkes. *Stop the FDA: Save Your Health Freedom.* Menlo Park: Health Freedom Publications, 1992.

Nussbaum, Bruce. *Good Intentions: How Big Business and the Medical Establishment Are Corrupting the Fight Against AIDS.* New York: The Atlantic Monthly Press, 1990.

Pauling, Linus C. *Vitamin C and the Common Cold.* New York: Bantam Books, 1971.

Rappoport, Jon. *AIDS Inc.—Scandal of the Century.* Foster City: Human Energy Press, 1988.

Shilts, Randy. *And the Band Played On: Politics, People and the AIDS Epidemic.* New York: St. Martin's Press, 1987.

Silverman, Milton and Philip R. Lee. *Pills, Profits and Politics.* San Francisco: University of California Press, Ltd., 1974.

The Burton Goldberg Group. *Alternative Medicine: The Definitive Guide.* Puyallup, Washington: Future Medicine Publishing, Inc., 1994.

Wilson, Jean D., M.D., and Daniel W. Foster, M.D. *Textbook of Endocrinology.* Philadelphia: W.B. Saunders Company, 1985.

Wright, Jonathan V., M.D. *Dr. Wright's Guide to Healing with Nutrition.* New Canaan: Keats Publishing, Inc., 1990.

GOVERNMENT PUBLICATIONS

Committee on Labor and Human Resources. *Dietary Supplement Health and Education Act of 1994.* 103d Congress, Report 103-410. October 1994.

CRS Report for Congress—July 15, 1993: Mortality Data Taken from U.S. Department of Health & Human Services, Centers for Disease Control & Prevention, National Health Statistics: Advance Report of Final Report of Final Mortality Statistics, 1990, *Monthly Vital Statistics Report,* v. 41, no. 7, Supplement, 7 January 1993.

Department of Agriculture. *Human Nutrition: Report No. 1—A Survey of Research on Human Nutrition Supported and/or Conducted by Public Research Organizations.* August 1971.

Department of Agriculture. *Human Nutrition: Report No. 2—Benefits from Human Nutrition Research.* August 1971.

FDA Dietary Supplements Task Force Final Report—June 1992. Released June 1993.

National Center for Health Statistics. *Healthy People 2000: National Health Promotion and Disease Prevention Objectives.* Maryland 1991.

NIH Nutrition Coordination Committee. *National Institutes of Health Program in Biomedical and Behavioral Nutrition Research and Training—Fiscal Year 1990.* No. 91-2092, September 1991.

United Kingdom. House of Commons. *Problems Associated with Aids.* Vol. III. Session 1986-1987.

U.S. Department of Health & Human Services. *Nutrition Research at the NIH.* No. 91-2611, September 1991.

MEDICAL JOURNALS

Bockman, Richard S., M.D., Ph.D. "Prostaglandins in Cancer: A Review." *Clin Sci Rev* 1 no. 6 (1983): 485-493.

Brush, M.G., Ph.D. "The Premenstrual Syndrome Before and After Pregnancy." *Maternal and Child Health* 10 (1985): 19-22.

Carter, James P., M.D. "Gamma-Linolenic Acid as a Nutrient." *Food Technology* (1988): 74-82.

Centers for Disease Control. "Epidemiologic Aspects of the Current Outbreak of Kaposi's Sarcoma and Opportunistic Infections." *NE J Med* 306 (1982): 248-252.

Concorde Coordinating Committee: "Concorde: MRC/ANRS Randomized Double-Blind Controlled Trial of Immediate and Deferred Zidovudine in Symptom-free HIV Infection": *The Lancet* 343 (1994): 871-880.

Das, U.N., M.D. "Antibiotic-like Action of Essential Fatty Acids." *Can Med Assoc J* 132 (1985): 1350.

———. "Can Essential Fatty Acid Deficiency Predispose to AIDS?" *Can Med Assoc J* 132 (1985): 900.

Donald, Alan. "Alcoholism: The Role of Essential Fatty Acids." *Bestways* (May 1987): 22-25.

Duffort, G., et al. "No Clinical Signs Fourteen Years After HIV-2 Transmission Via Blood Transfusion." *The Lancet* 2 no.8069 (1988): 510.

Fauci, Anthony S., M.D. "Acquired Immunodeficiency Syndrome: Epidemiologic, Clinical, Immunologic and Therapeutic Considerations." *Ann of Intern Med* 100 (1984): 92-106.

Graham, Neil, et al. "The Effects on Survival of Early Treatment of Human Immunodeficiency Virus Infection." *NE J Med* 326 (1992): 1037-1042.

Hales, Dianne. "How Fish Can Save Your Life." *Parade Magazine* (Nov 1986): 17.

Horrobin, David F. "Gamma-Linolenic Acid in Medicine." *1984-85 Yearbook of Nutritional Medicine* (1985): 23-35.

———. "Placebo-controlled Trials of Evening Primrose Oil." *Swed J Biol Med* 3 (1984): 13-17.

Horrobin, David F., and Mehar S. Manku. "Essential Fatty Acids in Clinical Medicine." *Nutrition and Health* 2 (1983): 127-134.

Horrobin, David F., and Y.S. Huang. "The Role of Linoleic Acid and Its Metabolites in the Lowering of Plasma Cholesterol and the Prevention of Cardiovascular Disease." *International J of Cardiology* 17 (1987): 241-255.

Horrobin, David F., et al. "Abnormal Essential Fatty Acid Levels in Plasma of Women with Premenstrual Syndrome." *Amer J Ob/Gyn* 150 (1984): 363-366.

———. "The Effects of Hydrogenated Coconut Oil and Evening Primrose Oil on Development of Hypertension and Sodium Handling in Spontaneously Hypertensive Rats." *Can J Physio Pharm* 63 (1985): 325-330.

———. "Patients with Primary Sjogren's Syndrome Treated for Two Months with Evening Primrose Oil." *Scand J Rheumatology* 15 (1986): 103-108.

Huang, C., et al. "Nutritional Status of Patients With AIDS." *Clinical Chemistry* 34 no. 10 (1988): 1957-1959.

Karmali, Rashida A., et al. "Effects of Dietary Enrichment with Gamma-Linolenic Acid Upon Growth of the R323OAC Mammary Adenocarcinoma." *J of Nutrition, Growth and Cancer* 2 (1985): 41-51.

Kromhout, Daan, et al. "The Inverse Relation between Fish Consumption and 20-Year Mortality from Coronary Heart Disease." *NE J Med* 312 (1985): 1205-1209.

Learment, J., et al. "Long-Term Symptomless HIV-1 Infection in Recipients of Blood Products from a Single Donor." *The Lancet* 340 no. 8824 (1992): 863-7.

Pulse, T.L., M.D., and Elizabeth Uhlig. "A Significant Improvement in a Clinical Pilot Study Utilizing Nutritional Supplements, Essential Fatty Acids and Stabilized Aloe Vera Juice in 29 HIV Seropositive, ARC and AIDS Patients." *J of Advancement in Medicine* 3 (1990): 209-230.

In addition to the above sources, the following journals and news magazines provided up-to-date information:

Alive, Alternative Medicine Digest, Citizens for Health Report, Delicious!, Faculty (Univ. of California, Berkeley), *Forbes, Health Foods Business, Health Freedom News, Health Freedom Reporter, Health Store News, Journal American, Let's Live, Los Angeles Reader, Ms., Newsweek, Scientific American, Spin, Sports Illustrated, Texas Monthly, The National Educator, Time, U.S. News & World Report, Vegetarian Times.*

What Health Professionals are Saying about
Innocent Casualties: The FDA's War Against Humanity

Read *Innocent Casualties* and get rightfully outraged by the FDA's inexcusable attack on American health. Feuer gives the reader ample and shocking documentation to make the case that our so-called food and drug regulatory office has become an "undercover dictatorship" specializing in police tactics.

Sandra Weinstein
Alternative Medicine Digest

Elaine Feuer goes where few dare to travel in her exciting exposé of the U.S. Food & Drug Administration. This is journalistic reporting the way it was meant to be!

Reality Press

Innocent Casualties is the perfect reference for the grassroots activist, as it provides the reader with documented evidence of recent FDA harassment and abuse of powers.

William H. Dailey, Esq.
Healthworld Online

Stories of FDA abuse of authority and conflict of interest abound in a controversial but thoroughly researched and documented new book by Elaine Feuer. *Innocent Casualties* reads like a crime thriller!

Barbara Clarke
Bodega Navigator

Elaine Feuer is an example of the proverbial "one person" that sometimes emerges from ordinary life to take on an injustice...*Innocent Casualties* uncovers the FDA's long-standing desire to put the entire nutritional supplement industry in the U.S. out of business, while at the same time allowing multinational pharmaceutical companies to sell dangerous prescription drugs.

Mark Conlan
Zenger's